Radiant Living

Holistic Coaches Share How Radiant Your Life Can Be

Anthology Compiled by Dez Stephens and
Co-Authored by Holistic Life Coaches
Trained by Radiant Health Institute
RadiantCoaches.com

Table of Contents

Moments Matter

by Suzie Kerr Wright

"The one wholly true thought one can hold about the past is that it is not here." (from A Course In Miracles*)*

This quote was delivered to my email as I was struggling with the topic for this passage. I wavered between several choices, as I often do. But as a fairly creative person, I wanted to write a chapter called, Creativity Matters. Yet I was repeatedly being reminded to stay in the present moment. I ignored that and kept looking for an angle, a way to approach the writing process and amaze you, dear reader, with my litany of talents and creative knowledge. But what I kept hearing in my head, my heart, and through other people-wherever I went was Now Matters and This Moment Matters. "Ahhh," I thought, "I should just stop and be in the moment to gain the appropriate inspiration for the amazing ideas I will impart on those less inspired than me." I thought I might take some time out of my busy schedule—later—and have a chat with God about how my contribution would go (read: rampant ego, spiritual procrastination and control). And then the quote appeared. This ego-driven human finally realized that God was sending me clear, concise messages repeatedly about what my topic should really be. Damn divine order. That was not my plan! Guess it was time for another spiritual lesson. Hrrrrmph!

"I don't have to force my spiritual practice on anybody, but I had better live it." ~ Caroline Myss

I am a woman who lives both in the past and future. I know I'm not alone in this behavior. Let me hear an "A-MEN!" I do cherish my past and hold onto a lot of family memorabilia. At the same time, being self-employed, I'm forever looking far ahead for the next opportunity to do...well, anything fun and potentially profitable. But as someone who has immersed herself in the practice and teaching of the Law of Attraction, I know better than to stay on either side of those worlds too long and risk abandoning what is now. I've seen my life go from the deepest, darkest depths of despair, loneliness, abuse, abandonment, and shame to the joy-filled life of purpose it is today. I could not have dreamed this life up, folks. As I stopped—yes, I finally did stop—to reflect on how it came to be, it was clear, and always has been and will be. It happened one moment at a time. Moments piled up one hour at a time, one day at a time, one year at a time.

"We will only understand the miracle of life fully when we allow the unexpected to happen. Every day, God gives us the sun - and also one moment in which we have the ability to change everything that makes us unhappy." - Paul Coelho

So just what is a moment? Here are two of the dictionary definitions:

1. Significant period: an important or significant time or occasion

2. Physics: product of force times distance: the product of a quantity such as a force multiplied by its perpendicular distance from a given point

The power of a single moment is often overlooked. In astrology, seconds matter when casting a chart. Just a few minutes' difference in the birth of twins will set up a completely different chart. That is one of the reasons why some twins don't look alike or act alike.

I find it interesting that the dictionary defines it as a "significant" time or occasion, and additionally, from a physics point of view, it is force multiplied by distance. We humans tend to forget or ignore the infinite power within our grasp. Science has proven our ability to influence our own lives and those of others. There is energy constantly being created and emitted by every one of us. Notice when you have had a strong, deep desire for something how your body tends to vibrate with intensity. You feel the thing you want. Your body reacts to what it will be like when you have this item in your hands or that person near you. You create the scenario—sights, sounds and smells—all in your mind and body.

Have you ever become frustrated, thinking really hard about how to do something, when someone interrupts your train of thought? You may let out a sigh or your body may suddenly relax. The point is you were creating a lot of energy. Just notice how much physical strength that took. Now imagine that energy of frustration going out into the world. What is it creating? The Law of Attraction is a constantly flowing gift from the Universe. Whether you believe you're creating energy or not, you are. Imagine if you took that force and allowed yourself to connect to the source for your highest and best.

"Whether you think you can, or you think you can't,

you're right". ~ Henry Ford

So let's just say for the sake of this article that a moment equals one second. It could realistically be more or less. Think about what a tenth of a second can mean to an Olympic athlete. It can mean the highest accolades or the pain of defeat. A moment could be that blip of time that passes as you hear devastating news that will change your life forever.

An old friend of mine, the late comedian Ron Shock, known as "America's Storyteller," videotaped his last months on earth in The Cancer Chronicles (on YouTube.com) so his friends and fans could share the victories and heartbreak with him. The support was overwhelming. The first video of the series began with him saying that on December 14, 2011 at 12:15pm, his doctor told him he had urethral cancer—one of the most aggressive and untreatable forms of cancer. He spoke of that very moment. He stated that up to

12:14pm on December 14th, he lived in one world. At 12:15pm, he suddenly lived in another. "A very scary world," he opined. He could not recall what he was thinking prior to hearing that diagnosis. Think about that for just a moment.

And what about the most beautiful and awe-inspiring moments—visions of nature that take your breath away, a simple statement of compassion from a loved one that opens your heart, an epiphany that propels you in the direction of your dreams, the "I do" at your wedding, the first "I love you" from your new love, or the brilliant idea that wakes you up in the middle of the night and fills you with excitement and adrenaline—blips in time but overwhelmingly powerful events that change you forever.

"Miracles come in moments. Be ready and willing." ~ Wayne Dyer

So how do you do this? What is staying in the

moment like? Is it difficult? Being present is easier than you think. I hear people say all the time that we're not wired to do this naturally, but actually we are. We're instinctual beings and our bodies provide us with vital information all the time. It's the outside influences that over-stimulate our senses or distract and disturb our energy. We allow this to happen. Staying present requires something that sounds like a dirty word to many of us. It's called discipline. It's the same as any acquired skill. It must be practiced.

Try this: set a period of time that you are willing to commit to this process. Choose whatever you're comfortable with. For example, let's start with one hour. Every 15 minutes in that hour, pause and look around you. What do you see? Don't think too much. Let worries, to-do lists and anxiousness all fade away for just 30 seconds. What do you feel? What do you hear? What do you smell? What do you taste? Notice your breathing. Pay attention to the ground you're standing on or the chair you're sitting in. You can do this anywhere. Stop your racing thoughts—therein lies the discipline. It helps if you set a timer initially so you won't keep worrying about how long it's been. Just breathe, see and feel. Pretty interesting, huh?

Before you resume your busy life, ask yourself, "What is the most amazing thing in this moment?" You might want to snap a picture of something that captures your attention—a flower, the sky, a pattern on a wall. Keep it with you to remind you of the freedom, peace, beauty and just plain awesomeness of being present for that short amount of time. You've just reset your internal operating system. Wow. That's called starting your day over.

"The Future is something which everyone reaches at the rate of sixty minutes an hour, whatever he does, whoever he is." ~ C.S. Lewis

There are 60 seconds in every minute, 3600

seconds in every hour, 86,400 seconds in every day and 31,536,000 seconds in every year. Each of these is as precious as the next. What are we doing with them? Each of these fragments of time is a grand opportunity—an opportunity to send out into the great Cosmic Galaxy a ray of hope, a vibration of love, a wave of forgiveness or a breath of fresh air. Force times distance. The thoughts we create each moment are propelling us into our own future. We're not there yet and we can't re-write the past. This second, this moment, oops it's gone. How about this one? Oops—gone again. You may have missed those fleeting increments of time, but the good news is you can begin again at any time. Right after you flip-off the jerk that cut you off in traffic. Just start over as often as you need to.

"The time to blossom is now, not sometime in the future when you believe the stars will be aligned for you." ~ Deepak Chopra

I hold the vision that the moments you spent reading these words gave you a more intimate and deeper appreciation for each breath of creation and assisted you in designing an exquisite future for yourself and this world.

Sharing of Yourself, Matters!

by Gina Kramer

What does it mean to be radiant, and to live a radiant life? The very basis of being radiant means to emit, shine, bring light, and joy. We each have a light, energy, knowledge, or power within ourselves that is meant to be shared. Let it shine. Let it emanate from your being—from every pore! When you shine, others will shine as well.

Your radiance—your inner light—is a gift that everyone is born with. Society, life experience, family, and friends teach us to hold back or extinguish that light. We learn to hide our light for fear of being hurt, criticized, or laughed at. It now seems odd to me that we are given a gift and then told not to unwrap it, to hide it and don't open it, and to not use it or even find out what it is. It's like giving a child a pretty wrapped package and telling them just to leave it in their closet without opening it. There is joy in seeing someone open a gift and in receiving a gift. In this case by opening your gift gives a gift to you and everyone you come into contact with. I don't imagine it was ever the intention that we were given a gift that we weren't meant to open and enjoy. Indeed, we're intended to allow others to enjoy our gift as well. Enjoy it, share it and allow it to grow and radiate.

In truth, we should be sharing that part of ourselves. When we allow ourselves to be radiant, it gives others permission to be radiant as well, bringing light, love, and joy to those around us. Opening ourselves causes a ripple effect. We share our radiance with those close to us, and all of those we come in contact with. They begin to share theirs with those close to them and so on until soon it becomes a visual radiance surrounding us—surrounding those we care for and love. The more we share, the more it grows. The more it grows the more powerful it becomes. The more lives we touch, the more legacy we leave behind.

There will always be those who wish to extinguish the light and radiance. Those who fear opening themselves to the possibilities will try to convince us to hide our light. They may be afraid of what might be seen in the light, afraid of change, afraid of opening themselves up to what might be, or afraid they will be hurt. Fear is our greatest barrier. We see our fear as a way to protect ourselves. In truth, it only binds us. It holds is where we are and keeps us from reaching our greatest potential.

Does it really matter why we have been taught to hide our light, or is it more important that we learn to shine and to help others shine as well? Maybe we are simply supposed to learn not to follow along like sheep and to be ourselves, reach out, emit our light, and our radiance. Maybe this is just part of the lessons of life. Maybe we are supposed to gain the strength to stand up and let our radiance shine. Whatever the reason, it's time to take a stand and become who we are meant to be. It's time to share ourselves and be powerful and shine brightly!

What is your radiance? What is within you that you should allow to shine and to benefit yourself and others? That radiance could be different for each person. It might be knowledge, ideas, love, energy, or a host of other possibilities. The only way to find your radiance is to open your gift. Open yourself to your instincts, to your light, and to the possibilities. What if sharing your radiance allows another person to open themselves and they become the next savant? They might become the person who ends poverty, hunger, or even brings world peace. You might become that person as well. Just think of all the possibilities. Whether you allow your light to shine or not, you touch the world and the lives of everyone you come into contact with. You have an effect—why not make it the most positive effect possible and make it have the largest impact possible?

One of my favorite quotes is from Marianne Williamson:

"Our deepest fear is not that we are inadequate. Our deepest fear is that we are powerful beyond measure. It is our light, not our darkness that most frightens us. We ask ourselves, 'Who am I to be brilliant, gorgeous, talented, fabulous?' Actually, who are you not to be? You are a child of God. Your playing small does not serve the world. There is nothing enlightened about shrinking so that other people won't feel insecure around you. We are all meant to shine, as children do. We were born to make manifest the glory of God that is within us. It's not just in some of us; it's in everyone. And as we let our own light shine, we unconsciously give other people permission to do the same. As we are liberated from our own fear, our presence automatically liberates others."

I think this quote says it best and states it very clearly. Each of us is meant to be powerful and brilliant. We are only taking away from ourselves and the world by hiding that brilliance. It is in everyone. We all have the ability. We all have so much more inside of ourselves than most of us ever realize. If we even suspect it's there, we are afraid to allow it to shine.

Why do we continue to hold ourselves back? Is it the psycho-babble we hear from the media, society, our friends, and family, or is it our own fear of failure or fear of great success? Are we afraid of making others feel small or insecure? If we open to our radiance what could that mean for us, for our families, our friends, and our world? What if opening ourselves allows others to do the same? What is the worst thing that could happen? What is the best thing? What amazing things could we accomplish? What could our world actually become?

Isn't it time to liberate yourself and become the person you want to be, or are meant to be? Allow yourself to be open to options and possibilities. Allow others to see your true self—your gifts, your talents, your light and all that you possess.

Now is the time to learn to shine and be radiant. Find the balance and happiness in your life. Let go of the fear. Let go of all the white noise and psycho-babble in your head. Let go of everyone else's opinion and find yourself. Find your voice, find your light, find what makes you different what makes you happy, find your joy, and let it shine. Be radiant.

How do you learn to shine? Different things work for different people. It's important to learn to trust your instincts. I think the most important thing is to accept that you are meant to be fabulous, brilliant, gorgeous, and talented. Face your fears, take down the barriers, and share yourself. There are numerous books, seminars, and classes that can be helpful to you. Encourage yourself as you would encourage others. Practice changing your self-talk, be positive, be happy, and make the choice to change yourself and your world. Look for others that share themselves and their light. Look for people you are drawn to—people who are upbeat and positive, who shine and are radiant. Surround yourself with people who are like the person you want to be—positive, helpful, people with a brilliance. Let the people go that want to hold you back or drag you down. It might help to explore new things that interest you. Talk to someone who can help you tap into who you really are, like a Life Coach. Learn to meditate to get in touch with your inner self. Learn to love yourself and learn to value yourself, your skills, and your gifts. Accept that you are important, that you make a difference. You have something to offer to others—something to offer the world that will make the world a better, brighter place.

Your radiance is a gift. It was and is a gift to you and it is your gift to others. You are not serving anyone by hiding your brilliance. You are actually keeping others from showing theirs as well. When you open to your gift and allow it to be a gift to all those who come into contact with you, then everyone will benefit form it. You will shine brighter and find more balance in your life. Be who you are meant to be, share your gifts, share your talents, share yourself, and be powerful beyond measure. **Let your radiance shine!**

Judgments, and lack thereof

by Teri Pugh

I'm always inspired and compelled to share the journey, and I believe that we each have these beautiful opportunities to do so. It just takes us choosing mindfulness and a willingness to slow down long enough in any given opportunity to be present and connect with others. When we do, something truly magical happens for those who believe in magic. Most skeptics are still curious, although outwardly they pretend otherwise. Nevertheless, internally a seed has been planted in our heart and a part of our soul awakened. I think we can all agree that if enough of the right seeds are planted or sowed, it is irrefutable that our harvest will be a beautiful and abundant. It will be a harvest of shared experience, valuable lessons, and wonderful pay-it-forward moments. Who doesn't want wonderful pay-it-forward moments? Here's to magic in motion and taking the opportunity to grow from our experiences and lay judgment to rest.

As I turned off of a somewhat busy road to enter the winding drive of the local grocery, I couldn't help but notice a young couple and their three dogs. The guy was holding a sign which read, "Headed to Philly, any help is appreciated." I'm not even going to lie, being an animal lover and animal rights advocate, my initial thought was, "those poor dogs out in this heat are probably hungry and thirsty. Who does that to their pets?" Immediately, I noticed my preconceived judgment and I knew it was unwarranted. I did not know them, I did not know their story, and I certainly was in no position to judge. I realigned my thought, embracing the young traveling couple, and I wondered how they ended up here, in Nashville.

I parked and entered the bustling store. I could not help but notice that the chattering around me seemed muted compared to the voice in my head, which continually bounced a multitude of probing questions back and forth about the young couple that seemed to occupy my brainwaves. As I began to shop, I simply could not get them out of my mind. I was curious about them and their story. I worried for them and their dogs and soon noticed that with every item I put in my cart, recurring thoughts arose. I wondered—Are they hungry? Are they thirsty? What's their story? Were they really headed to up to Philly? I will confess, I have often wondered silently in my mind when I have seen people with signs asking for help on the sides of the streets if they were simply pit stopping along an adventurous journey or if it was a manipulating ploy for sympathy and fast cash to fuel an unhealthy lifestyle. Whatever the reasons, it is not my journey, nor is it my place to judge. As I made my way down the snack isle, without thinking, I was picking up granola bars, then Gatorade, water, a bag of apples, and before I knew it, I was reasoning with myself over how much they could carry and what would or would not spoil in the intolerable heat.

Next, I twisted and turned my way through the store, navigating to the pet food. Another dilemma ensued—dry food, wet food, how much, puppy or adult. Food, a few flea collars, and a bag of treats later, I had a mostly full basket of goodies for my still unknown traveling friends. How is it that people I have never met other than with a glance from a distance could consume my thoughts? Perhaps it was a divine intervention—an opportunity for me to rethink my old knee jerk habit of "assuming" something. We all know what they say about assuming. I continued on, noticing that I'd not picked up even one item I had initially gone to the store for, but I was okay with that. We have two dogs of our own and I knew, if nothing else, I could not come home without a surprise for them. So, I picked up a party of five of the weekly XL Dentabones, tossed them in my cart, and proceeded back to the food section to at least pick up a few must-haves for our home. By now, I had successfully bought our groceries for the week and a supply of goodies which I had hoped would be well received by the young couple and their dogs, so I hurried out to the car, hoping they had not picked up and moved on.

There, behind a slew of cars in the turning lane, I spotted them resting under a shade tree. I pulled off the road and called out to them, asking if they were okay with me giving their dogs some food and water. They replied in a very free-spirited and appreciative way, "Sure thanks!" as smiles crossed their sun-kissed faces. This was someone's daughter, someone's son—a young couple, I would say in mid-to-late twenties. They stood up among their scattered backpacks, bottled waters and Thomas the Train blanket to greet me and quickly thanked me again as I handed their adorable pups, named Cowboy, Blue, and Otis, the treats. I explained I'd bought them a few items as well and handed them a canvas bag full of nutrition and two gallons of water. They were most appreciative and asked if I'd like to sit with them for a while. It was as though they were inviting me into their living room. Technically, I guess you could say they were. So, I sat.

Our conversation began with the dogs—I heard the story of how they came to be a family by rescuing homeless dogs because they couldn't bear to think of them living on the streets alone with no family. Ironic? No, actually. Both these kids had homes— Philly for the guy and Chicago for the girl. Their families while not fully supportive or even remotely excited about their traveling life, but did love them and kept in touch when they could. Our conversation touched on the love they had for their dogs. Being the crazy animal advocate that I am, I was compelled to mentioned flea and heartworm prevention, at which moment Blue walked clumsily across a duffel bag to come to me. As he gracefully stepped all over the duffle bag, I heard the familiar sound of squeaky toys. In fact, that duffel bag was packed with toys, water bowls, flea collars, shampoo and vitamins. I mentioned one of my fellow animal advocates, whose mission it is to regularly check in on the well-being of the local homeless folks and their pets. The girl quickly spoke up, asking me if I knew the lady on the street downtown who plays the spoons, further explaining that they had passed through downtown last night and met some super nice folks. One such person was the spoon lady, who had told them about the very animal advocate to whom I was referring—small world.

Our conversation went on to the young man's education. After finishing a state college with a Bachelor of Arts, he decided he wanted to travel. He was not big on corporate life, so he followed his heart, packed a bag, and hit the road, hitching rides with folks in cars or seeing the country complements of an open boxcar on a train. He couch surfed and slept under the stars, and said, for the most part, people were very friendly. The young man wore broken specs, cut off camouflage pants, and was barefoot with a fedora. He was looking forward to taking his dog Cowboy down to the nearby creek for an opportunity to swim as Otis and Blue napped under the tree. He commented that he planned to get Cowboy a new collar, as his current one didn't have a metal ring for his tags and local police give him a hard time about that. I mentioned that I probably had one in my car. Low and behold, not only did I have one collar, I had two, two leashes, and a tennis ball— imagine that. Our conversation bounced from nutritional facts to dogs not having the ability to sweat, from pet overpopulation to organic farming, from politics to favorite music—Freddie Fender and the Mama's and the Papa's—didn't see that coming. What a bright, caring couple who travel the U.S. via railroad cars! And yes, in fact, they were headed back to Philly to stay the through the winter with family. Fast forward an hour later and it was time for me to hit the road. They thanked me again for sitting with them and for the kindness. I truly enjoyed them and I'm thankful to have met them. I could have doubted their story or I could have kept driving after seeing them and thought to myself that they were nothing more than what some call panhandlers, but then I would have missed out on a wonderful conversation with some pretty remarkable folks.

The lesson in this experience for me personally was simply a reaffirming of what I know to be true. We are all wonderful, brilliant beings and we each have our own unique story to share. Most of all, there truly are folks who are willing, if not eager, to get to know us for who we are. I believe that as easy and effortlessly as it seems for many of us to judge others by our own set of standards and life experiences, it is just as easy to adjust our perception and our thought, embracing others and tapping into our natural element of compassion, kindness, and generosity. It truly is a win-win for all.

Dao of Meditation

by David Patterson

"No problem can be solved from the same level of consciousness that created it" - *Einstein*

In my personal opinion, meditation is "medication" for the mind. Though I myself am far from what some may perceive as an "enlightened yogi," I can definitely attest to the fact that even a little meditation regularly, in whatever form you so choose to meditate, can greatly impact your life in a very noticeable and positive way. There is a quote by an unknown person that goes something like, "There are many different roads, but they all lead to Me." Though that quote has been used in many different scriptures worldwide, I think when applied to the art of meditation, it fits perfectly. There are many different methods to meditate, many breathing patterns, gestures, taboos, and so forth that aid in achieving a serene state of being, but there is probably no "ultimate" way. So try not to get caught up on what is deemed "superior" or what some guru or accomplished spiritual master has done to obtain enlightenment. In doing so, not only will you miss the lesson, but you will likely not enjoy the journey to your destination. So, let me begin introducing a form of meditation that has worked for me, share a brief story of how I even began to meditate, and how, on a very mundane level, it helped me live a more radiant life.

About five years or so ago, I was in a wonderful relationship with a young woman, whom I thought I would one day marry. Everything between us seemed to fit so symmetrically. And one day, just as magically as it began, it abruptly ended. To make matters worse, I found the news that she was engaged to be married to another suitor through a third party. Auugh! I was devastated. I went through periods of denial, then anger, then pain. It got to the point where almost every song that played on the radio seemed to rub it in my face. I kept running into people we both knew personally that were just so shocked we had broken up and who asked me a billion unanswerable questions. My mind would just not leave the thought alone. I would eventually quit my boxing class that I was taking, which I originally joined with her in our pursuit to live a more radiant life together. I could not even find the energy to entertain the many suitors that came my way because all I could see was "her" in them. I even quit exercising, which for me was huge. I am by nature a gym rat. I personally feel more at home in the gym than at home. I knew something must be done, and was open to whatever came my way. Finally, lightning struck.

I knew the first step to me recovering from this heart ache was to quiet the nagging thoughts that seemed to run endlessly through my mind. I stumbled across a meditation technique known to some in Sanskrit as Trataka which is the technique of fixing one's eyes upon the flame of a candle for any given amount of time to help develop focus, concentration, and even awaken the inner vision. What initially interested me in this particular form of mediation was that when you practice Trataka, it can calm the mind, deepen breath, increase the ability to concentrate, provide a "natural high," and allow one to develop a heightened sense of self awareness and insight. After about seven minutes of focusing on one thing, your brain gets bored with all the random thoughts and inner chatter that it is accustomed to and tends to quiet down and focus on what is in front of you. For me, it sounded perfect, so I found a small tea light candle and focused on the steady flicker of the flame until I could no longer hear my self think. It was amazing for me the first time I practiced this technique—I could literally feel the mental debris leave my mind, which did not, however, take away the emotional pain that was felt. But, it did take away the thoughts that made me re-live these emotions that I wanted to be liberated from.

Below is a small walk through this form of

meditation. Feel free to add or subtract what works best for you. I have tried this meditation with a flame, a quartz crystal, a black dot, a spiritual yantra, and a tree—all with pleasing results. For this example, we will concentrate on a flame.

Step 1. Sitting comfortably in a straight back chair, take three deep breaths, relaxing your mind and body. Do not try to control your breath—simply become aware of it. Let your breath inhale and exhale naturally on its own. You will slowly begin to relax. Let your thoughts come and go as they please. Do not make any attempt to control them.

Step 2. Now, gaze at the flame with a relaxed gaze, almost as if you are looking through or past the flame. Continue breathing in a deepened, relaxed manner. Focus more on your breathing than on the quietness of your mind, allowing the thoughts to come and go as they please without judging or engaging your self in them.

Step 3. After a few moments of this, your mind should begin to get bored. It will become easier to focus on the flame without any interference from your mind. Just sit in this state for three to five minutes at the beginning and gradually work your way up to fifteen to thirty minutes or more daily. When you are done, wiggle your fingers and toes to bring awareness to your body again. The objective at this point is consistency. Some other reported benefits of this exercise include a heightened ability to focus, strengthened eye muscles, increased will power, and more lucid dreams.

Now that I found a way to shift my focus away from the negative thought pattern that I had developed, I had to find a way to release the negative emotions that I still possessed. I needed something that would aid me throughout the day, to help me quiet the thoughts of "her" I had throughout my waking life.

Sound frequencies can be a very powerful therapeutic form of redirecting and calming thought energy and encouraging healing. Shamans and other practitioners of various ancient tribal techniques would use heavy drums made of natural fibers that they would play continuously for hours to help a person achieve a heightened state of awareness. This is sometimes necessary to "go within," to divine for healing remedies, or just to enjoy a euphoric trance-like state. Drumming is just one of many ways to achieve a deeper meditative state. Chanting mantras or reciting words of power is another.

At some point in my quest to achieve inner peace, I was lead to a simple mantra that I have used to help my mind and body feel at ease and at peace in a way I had not quite experienced until that point. There are many mantras that come form all parts of the globe, but my mantra of choice at this time was "aum" or "om." Now, when I stumbled across this, I had no idea that it would even work.

Actually, I was a bit skeptical of my seemingly unorthodox approach to my problem, but what did I have to lose? You cannot exactly take medicine for a broken heart, so this was my best option.

Step 1. Find a comfortable place to sit in an upright fashion. Close your eyes and take three deep breaths, really slowly inhaling and really slowly exhaling. When you inhale, stick your stomach out, away from your spine. When you exhale, try to breathe all the air out of your lungs. Pause a second and repeat the cycle.

Step 2. After your third inhale you want to exhale "om," pronounced like: "OOOOOOOOOOMMMMMMMMMMMMMMMM," followed by a pause. And during the inhale silently say to your self: "OOOOOOOMMMMMMMMM," followed by another pause. Repeat this cycle for at least seven or so times at the beginning and then increase the repetitions with more practice. You might feel tingles, body sensations, natural highs, an increase sense of awareness, and more vivid dreams among other things as a result of regular practice, but don't be discouraged if you don't experience any of the above. Each individual has their own experience.

Step 3. After you are done, open your eyes and become aware of where you are. Wiggle your fingers and toes to begin to bring more awareness to your body. As with all forms of meditation and self cultivation, consistency is the key. This is a simple meditation with many benefits, and some that you can only understand after you have experienced the technique.

This single exercise worked so well for me that what began as a ten to thirty minutes of practice quickly escalated to sixty minutes and then two hours a day. I was meditating on "om" so consistently that my body actually began to feel like it was floating. I felt alive. I felt wave after wave of peace upon my being. Even during my waking hours, I felt what I could only describe as a "natural high." It was odd to me that something as simple as a mantra could cause such a noticeable positive impact on my life. I even began to question why I had even spent so much time dwelling in the negative thoughts of my ended relationship. With my new mind-state of peace and serenity, I didn't even care anymore. I began to find pleasure in some of the smallest things, like walking outside, listening to water run in nature, listening to birds sing, and even the wind seemed to me to feel different caressing against my skin. *I was a new man*. Even my co-workers sensed the change. People would often tell me that they felt a sense of peace just being around me. I found it easier to eat healthier—it was almost like I made no conscious effort on my part. I picked up drawing and painting again, which seemed to flow easier than before. I began to write poetry again. I found it easier to express myself. In some ways, I was literally on top of the world inside. Now, I don't claim to know the complete science or biochemical changes a body undergoes from chanting, but I will tell you that sometime after the second or third week of regular meditation of about one hour or longer in the morning and before bed, I began to change. It was amazing.

Some years later it was revealed to me that though I had accomplished much in my meditating practices, I still had one task to overcome—forgiveness. At this time, I had not thought much of my ex at all. I had no anger, resentment, or regrets of which I was aware. I even wondered why I was somehow being led to forgive her when I had not thought about her in over three years. However, this next meditative exercise that I recommend is probably, in my opinion, the most important. It is known to some as "cord cutting." What is cord cutting you ask? Well, in my opinion, it is a method of subconsciously, energetically cutting away or releasing all that is attached to you that no longer serves you at this time. The cutting happens on the inner levels within you during a meditative state.

Afterwards, the results can be felt on a physical level of your being, usually through a lightness of the body, a sensation of release throughout the body, especially the area of the heart, or just a feeling of relief may be felt. During the process, some have been reported to cry, laugh, dream, or even re-live the situations one last time as they are being released. The results vary. This simple exercise may work wonders in your life and can be adapted to benefit whatever works for you. If there is a person or habit you want to release, or just forgiveness you want to ask of yourself or another, this is a perfect exercise. The beautiful thing is that the thing in question doesn't even have to be present for the technique to work. They don't even have to be still alive for that matter. The possibilities are endless.

This particular exercise has two parts. The first part consists of you relaxing your entire body to deepen your state of trance. The second consists of a visualization of the actual cord cutting process.

Part 1.

Step 1. You want to find a place where you can lie down or sit comfortably in a straight backed chair. Begin by taking three deep inhalations and exhalations. Take slow, long, deep breaths. Now, imagine that you are surrounded by a white light that engulfs and protects your entire body from head to toe.

Step 2. Begin first at your toes and feet by saying to yourself, "relax toes, relax feet, relax toes, relax feet, relax." At the same time, imagine warming energy surging gently to your toes and feet. Repeat this at least three times, slowly.

Step 3. Now, do the same for your lower legs and calves. Say to yourself, "relax calves, relax leg, relax calves, relax legs, relax." At the same time, send warming energy to your calves and legs. Repeat this process slowly at least three times. Slowly work your way all the way up the body, hitting all the major body parts. By the time you get to your head and eyes, you should feel pretty relaxed.

Part 2.
Step 1. Now that you are completely relaxed, take yourself to a place in your imagination that feels safe and serene for you. It can be anything—a garden, a place in nature, a waterfall—it does not matter. Be creative!

Step 2. Now imagine the person or object that you would like to release standing there in front of you. Imagine this person looking at you with eyes of unconditional love and understanding. Imagine energetic cords that run from all parts of your body, the most prominent of which connects your heart center to this person's body.

Step 3. Tell the person of interest all the things that you despise about them. Tell them all the things that you never got to express, all the things that made you sad, hurt, and irate. Tell them everything that you always wanted to say! Tell them everything.

Step 4. Now tell them all the things about them that you loved. Tell them about how much you learned from them and how they helped your grow into the person you are today. Tell them all the good things and thank them for their relationship with you.

Step 5. Now ask them to forgive you for all of your wrongdoing in the relationship. Then tell them that you forgive them as well, and at this time you would like to release them and set them free to live their own life in a way that was best for them. Step 6. Imagine in your hands are a giant sword, knife, or pair of scissors infused with golden light. Take your sword and begin to hack away at all the cords that connect you and this other person. Feel the emotions being released with each cord that is cut. Keep in mind that you are not releasing this person in your life from you completely, just releasing the unhealthy or unwanted aspects of the relationship. Cut away at all the cords leaving the one that connects at the heart for last. Now, with one final blow, hack away at the giant cord that connects you at the heart.

Step 7. Now look into the eyes of the person you have called before you. Do they look relieved? Do you feel lighter? Thank them one last time for all the lessons they have imparted to your life. Now release them one last time. When you are ready, slowly come back into awareness with your body and your environment. How do you feel? Keep in mind that sometimes the pain is buried deep and it may take a few sessions to completely let go. Also know that you can alter this exercise in anyway that suits you to meet your individual needs.

After my first time doing this exercise, I felt a profound overall difference in my being. I felt light as a feather. To my surprise, I actually felt the sensation of something leaving my chest during the meditation. My breathing deepened and I felt that I had truly accomplished something worthwhile. It changed my life. I felt that more color had come into my world—it was simply amazing. After waking the next morning feeling refreshed and renewed, I received a call to contact a young lady who was looking to employ a male licensed massage therapist. Even my financial situation began to change for the better after the cord cutting meditation. To top it off, the same young woman I was to contact would later become a very close friend, life mate, and spiritual partner, who I would share a very harmonious relationship with. I have a theory that until I was able to release the hurt and un-forgiven grief from my previous relationship, I would not have been ready to enjoy such a beautiful soul, such as herself. This is my testimony of how meditation changed my life permanently and helped me live a more radiant and abundant life.

I would like to end on a quote by author and

businessman Stephen Covey. "Every human has four endowments—self awareness, conscience, independent will, and creative imagination. They give us the ultimate human freedom...The power to choose, to respond, to change".

For a More Radiant Life – Connection
by Lori Bradford Miles

It is through connection and intimacy that we as human beings can live a more radiant life. Connection means a relation of personal intimacy, or a means of communication.

The Universe responds to the vibrations we emit through our thoughts words and actions. As we find connection with ourselves, this moves to our relationships and then the whole world—all creatures and beings on the planet and within the entire Universe. One thing that unites us together is that we all long to be happy. This happiness usually includes the desire to be close to someone in a loving or intimate way. Draw upon your own inner-resources to offer love, attention, and sustenance to yourself when you need it. Then you can let love come to you instead of putting expectations on what it needs to look like. Genuine happiness is not about feeling good about ourselves because other people love us—it's more about how well we have loved ourselves and others. The unintentional outcome of loving others more deeply is that we are loved more deeply. In order to accept that love can't rescue you from being alone, learn to spend time being with yourself. By feeling safe and secure to be on your own within the framework of relationship, you will feel more complete, happy, and whole.

Spiritual Connection

Ancient wisdom describes human beings as having five layers of experience: the environment, the physical body, the mind, the intuition, and our self or spirit. If our environment is clean and positive, it has a positive impact on all the other layers of our existence. As a result, they come into balance and we experience a greater sense of peace and connection within ourselves and with others around us. The properties of the Universal Mind are omniscience (all knowing), omnipotence (all powerful), omnificence (all creative) and omnipresence (always present). Know that this too is your nature. You have access to all knowledge, known and unknown. You have access to an infinite power, for which nothing is impossible. You have access to the limitless creativity of the One Creator. All these attributes are present within you at all times in their potential form. Beliefs about the origin of the universe are at the root of our consciousness as human beings. To live spiritually means you have connected with your source energy. Once you have connected with divine source energy, you are at peace with yourself and the world around you. We are living in a time where we are experiencing spiritual awareness worldwide. We are becoming aware that there is something more than our physical bodies and that we are an extension of divine source energy. We all have threads of energy that are our own frequency, and that frequency can change throughout our lives.

Prayer Movement and Meditation Connection

Set an intention for each day as an embodied prayer while you make a list what you have to be grateful for. Reading books, writing, or journaling can be used for problem-solving and stress reduction. These practices have been proven to improve mental and physical health. They can lead to increased self-esteem. Write down your thoughts. Sometimes books can touch on your emotions, or serve as a reminder you of your own life as part of the larger human experience.

Take a walk and breathe to put the serenity back into your mind and thoughts. Everyone can get in touch with their inner musical self and create prayer through music—whether it is listening to your favorite songs, chanting, or creating your own music. Try movement, walking, running, dancing, doing yoga, or just being open to new experiences, new people, and places. Notice the sacred in and around you. Uncovering your spirituality may take some self-discovery.

Gratitude Connection

This connection is a daily expression of finding gratitude, focused on the rich blessings of "what's now." If you're open to it, it brings you into the present moment immediately. Gratitude sends the vibrational message of connection to others that are alike in our consciousness, and leads us to that place of joy in our hearts. Expressing gratitude deepens the experience and meaning of it by creating a gratitude connection. When we "do thanks," we connect, and when we connect, we become more loving. When we practice gratitude each day, there will be a shift toward bringing happiness and well being into a new light. The emotion we feel when we experience Gratitude feels like we are loved unconditionally and aligned to self.

Nature Connection

Nature has its own means of balance. If you

observe nature, you will see that the five elements that form its basis are opposed to each other. We learn from nature how to balance opposing forces, both within ourselves and in the world around us. Humans have a deep need to connect with nature. When we connect with nature, we connect with the larger whole, energizing and inspiring. The natural environment helps us recognize our oneness with the life process. Taking us beyond our limited and linear view of life, nature celebrates growth and perpetual renewal. No matter how much we work on ourselves spiritually, the food we eat does plays a very significant role on feelings, mindfulness, appreciation, connection, love, intimacy, and socializing. Food is a energetic source which interacts with humans on the physical level, the emotional level, and also the energetic and spiritual levels. Since the beginning of time, food has nourished us multi-dimensionally. There is an interdependence and connection among plants, animals, humans. Spending time in nature is a blessing in itself. Nature supports the mind-body connection. Walking with a friend through nature is a way of sharing of spiritual expression that can help build relationships with one's self or with others. One of the lessons that nature teaches us is about how we relate to the natural world. After spending time in nature, the actual moment, the present, re-establishes itself. This is deeply nourishing for the soul, and relaxing for the mind and body, and allows stress to effortlessly dissipate. There are countless ways to connect and recharge with Mother Nature. Their quiet, rhythmic qualities are especially soothing. They require a sharpening of the senses and the sensibilities. You learn to better use your ears, eyes, sense of smell, and balance. In a sense, we become more alive when we become more mindful and present. When we are truly centered in the life-current flowing through us, we tend to act in ways that promote the well being and harmony of the whole. Our connection with the Mother Universe makes it possible for all human beings to come into collective alignment.

Relationship Connection

Relationships are more than just satisfaction with human connections. The more you feel that you have a purpose in the world, the less solitary you feel—even when you're alone. Connection is action that puts humans in contact with each other. Connection is the knowledge that we are loved by God. This frees us to love others more genuinely. In this wholeness, we can create real intimacy, get in touch with the spaciousness in one's own heart, and bring awareness to the light. It is in our nature as human beings to want to be close to and valued by others consistently over time. We are naturally drawn to people whose frequencies are harmonious with our own. Others who are on similar paths can also merge energies and visions through their interconnectedness.

The people we connect with in these ways are "kindred spirits", and they are "like souls" of what could be called our vibration tribe or stream. Cultivating your spirituality may help uncover what's most meaningful in your life, developing your own sense of purpose. We begin to celebrate the experience of differences in relationships and rejoice in the feeling of oneness in the essential true nature of love. This opens the door for learning from one another, sharing wisdom and growing together in harmony. In holistic, healthy relationships, the exchange of energy is balanced and reciprocal. When you feel part of a greater whole, you realize that you can share the burdens as well as the joys of life with those around you. Whatever the adversity or learning experience may be, it will move you to a higher level of spirituality once you open your heart, and you will connect more easily with source energy.

"A human being is part of the whole called by us universe, a part limited in time and space. We experience ourselves, our thoughts and feelings as something separate from the rest. A kind of optical

delusion of consciousness. This delusion is a kind of prison for us, restricting us to our personal desires and to affection for a few persons nearest to us. Our task must be to free ourselves from the prison by widening our circle of compassion to embrace all living creatures and the whole of nature in its beauty. The true value of a human being is determined by the measure and the sense in which they have obtained liberation from the self. We shall require a substantially new manner of thinking if humanity is to survive." – Albert Einstein

Forgiveness: The Next Generation

by Karen Kipke

The day I became a mother was the most blessed day of my life. I was scared to death! I had absolutely no idea what to do with this fragile creature before me. Nonetheless, this day was the day I had felt the most love inside me, the most love surrounding me, and the most love emanating from that precious little body. I felt love as a giver of complete, unconditional love. I finally understood what the word unconditional meant.

Often when we are on the receiving side of love, it is a love of conditions. Essentially, these conditions result in painful love. This damaged love is excruciating to break through once it has been absorbed into the heart. The heart actually becomes broken, for conditional love weakens the body and creates disease in us all.

Oh baby! Toddlers can kick better than a soccer

player. Toddlers can bite better than great white sharks, leaving you with teeth marks as a souvenir. Toddlers can scream louder than a sonic boom! Toddlers can hit harder than a prize fighter who just won the Heavyweight title. And, best of all, they can throw temper tantrums that would land them perfect tens from a panel of Olympic judges. If you weren't already at your wit's end with your angel baby acting this way, it always seems to be in public. What a cruel, cruel joke.

What is a mother to do when her darling daughter crawls out from under the bathroom stall at the Aquarium, lies down on the disgusting bathroom floor, (you know, the one that you can just see the germs jumping up from the ground onto her body—I can just hear my mother now) and wails her pretty little head off, leaving one caught with pants down and no choice but to charge out of the stall to gather this dead weight child for fear that she will get gobbled up from all the baby snatchers lurking around the corner. Meanwhile, one gets looks of disapproval from all the friendly bathroom guests. Then, baby girl sprints right out of the bathroom into her daddy's arms, not a tear in sight, and is once again a sweet princess while the mother feels completely defeated as the tears well up in her eyes, husband helpless, for he knows not what just happened.

When you find yourself as a parent, guardian, or friend on the receiving end of this spiteful love, receive it. Yes, receive it. Accept that your child is frustrated. If you think you are frustrated with all of your coping skills you have as an adult, realize that your little one feels one hundred times more frustrated than you do this very moment. Understand that he is having great angst in communicating his needs. Know that this is when your child needs you the most. Receive their pain with love in your heart. Know that your child is looking to you for guidance and is in need of love—your best love.

Give to your child without judgment, fear, or discipline. Give from that most blessed first day of motherhood. Give from deep within your heart. We all vow we will do better as parents than our parents did. Prove it. Prove it in this emotionally charged moment of turmoil. Prove that you are a giver of unconditional love. Believe that what your child is crying for is your love. Take a deep breath, reach out your arms, and fill the space with loving kindness.

Before you close your eyes this evening, forgive yourself. Forgive yourself for the ugly stares you received in the bathroom stall. Forgive yourself for not having the superhuman power to translate the mysterious temper tantrum language. Forgive yourself for being the worst mother in the world.

Know there will be many more days of joyous ups and those dreadful downs. Forgive yourself for mistakes to come. Absolve yourself from your "sins." Allow compassion to find space in your heart for that beautiful love to exude as it is meant to.

With all the lessons we wish to teach our children, the ultimate lesson is self-love. No money in the world can buy self-love. No noble beings can give you self-love, but self-love can be observed, and you as a parent are the role model.

I invite you to close your eyes for a moment and imagine a world full of self-love.

What does it look like for generations to come? Do you wish to live there? You can!

You will live on in the souls of generations to come. Your spirit will live on as self-love. This is your legacy.

A Lotus's Journey from the Muck

by Katie Slachciak

It amazes me to look back at myself ten years ago and see how much I have evolved. My outlook on life has become so positive and full of love. My spiritual self has been reborn—I feel like I am in the toddler stage of my spirituality. By that, I mean I am full of energy and a sponge for knowledge. A decade ago I thought I knew everything, and yet I was scared and didn't even know who I was. My tale of emergence from these mucky waters began in 2003, when I was eighteen years old.

To say it was mucky is not an understatement. I had no direction or guidance. Imagine being so deep in the dark waters that you have no idea which way is up or down. I had no spiritual connections and was pretty good at not being open with people. I was on medication for depression, panic attacks, and general anxiety. My late teens and early twenties were speckled with relationships that never lasted. They were great until that six-month mark—at that time I would quickly find things I did not like about them, or I would put my wall up. One of these relationships gave me my oldest son. I was nineteen years old and knew my life was about to change for the better. When a life changing event knocks on our door, we always have to choose how we are going to handle it. When you choose to embrace this sudden change as a blessing, it is as if you slingshot yourself on to a brand new path. With faith that "everything will work out" comes results, and everything will work out! I was nineteen years old and decided to embrace responsibility. This is when I realized which direction was up.

Fast forward two years. I was twenty-two years old with a two-year old son, had recently quit both jobs, and dropped out of college. I knew I wanted a job that could give me a sense of purpose. I wanted a house for my son and I, and I wanted to surround myself with happy friends. I know now that by setting those goals, I actually slingshot these events and people to the Universe! At this point, I felt like I was so close to the surface of the water. I could see the light shining through, but it was still out of reach. It was as if I was waiting for someone to reach in and pull me out. I was done waiting! Something shifted inside of me and I became engulfed with my own power! When this shift happened, I exploded from underneath the water and could finally take that huge breath of air that I needed so desperately. This is when I decided to pack up my son, along with everything that we could fit into my little Elantra, and move down to Tennessee to start a new life.

I had never felt this feeling before! I was so empowered by my courage—I knew only great things would be in store for us. When I arrived in Tennessee, I had a job waiting for me. It was a job I looked forward to everyday and I met new, fun friends. They were the type of friends that I could be myself around. Two months after living here, my son and I moved into our very own house! I got everything I wanted by taking my life into my own hands and accepting help from people who offered. Our thoughts control our emotions and the direction of our path. The longer you hang on to negative thoughts and feelings, the longer it will be until you are able to embark on the new path that waits ahead of you. It does not take special people with magical gifts to do amazing things in this world. We all have the potential! It was one thing for me to want these changes, but they were not going to happen until I shifted my thoughts. Once I did, all the doors opened up for me. At this point in my life, I had completely emerged from those mucky, dark waters to become a lotus bud, floating on the surface.

We are really going to fast forward now to 2012. I am twenty-seven years old, have two more sons, and am divorced from the father of my first son. Deciding to get a divorce was another empowering moment in my life. The whole marriage felt like an anchor that was holding me back from being who I was supposed to be. One day, I envisioned two roads—road A was being married, and road B was getting a divorce. Road A was cloudy and felt suffocating. Road B was sunny, bright, and it was so easy to breathe! It was in that moment that I decided I was going to get a divorce to get my freedom back and to live my happiness. I was not worried about how I was going to pay for it or how I was going to support my three kids. I knew that money would come someway. I knew that God would take care of the kids and I because I was going to do this for us.

I was once asked, "How do you hug little Katie?" Um, how do I what? They rephrased, "How do you show yourself love?" I thought about it and responded, "I don't." Then I cried. I was so consumed with doing things for other people in my life that I forgot about myself! This person explained to me that we need to make ourselves the top priority in our own lives. If I could find time for a friend who was in need, then I should be able to squeeze myself into my day, too. I made a vow to myself right then to show myself love every day. This is when I began my spiritual awakening! The lotus bud begins to open...

Do you ever get tired of those "Negative Nancy's" in your life? When I chose to move to Tennessee, I had them. When I chose to get a divorce, they were there too. I believed in my power so much that I was able to hush "Nancy" up. It seems when you let Nancy into your plans too much, she will throw you off track. One thing I have learned about change is that it sometimes comes with transitional setbacks. Changes are our spiritual evolutions. When a setback occurs, this is when we build and strengthen our spiritual muscles. It takes courage and willpower to push through these moments, but we just have to remember what our final outcome will be! Keeping that end result in the front of our brain will help give us that drive to see the change through.

I had a surprise setback about six months after my divorce was final. My boss came to me and told me she was cutting my hours to part-time. Then, two months later, I was completely laid off. As a single mother of three little boys, I had to do something—but what? There were two options in that situation—crawl into a hole of despair, blaming the employer, or see this as a gift to start a new path! Don't get me wrong, I cried and was angry and scared for a couple of days. I made the choice to stop all that nonsense and see this as a blessing. I knew somehow the kids and I would be taken care of, and that this was a great opportunity. I didn't like the job I had anyway. I had no passion for what I did there. I remember thinking I wanted a change a few months prior to being let go, and I wanted to be self-employed. I wanted to do something that made a difference in a person's life and to feel pride in my work. By focusing my energy and thoughts on framing my situation in a positive light, amazing things have resulted.

I see myself now as a beautifully blossomed lotus, full of gratitude and pride for where I have traveled to get where I am. So many roads lay ahead of me, new paths that I have not even thought of yet! I am ready to embrace new challenges and embrace the new people that will enter my life. Perhaps my purpose is to share my journey with others to help empower them in their lives. If I were asked to sum it all up and offer a young woman some words of wisdom, I would say something like this:

For starters, feel everything to the fullest, the good and the bad. The bad things like heartbreak or losing a job are going to suck, and hurt! But, if you live that pain you will be able to walk away with your lesson. If we bottle up those feelings, they may come back to haunt us later. So let those feelings come up and run their course. Pay special attention to the hard times because that is where you will learn the best lessons. For every tragic event, heartbreak, and bad decision I have made, there has been a lesson learned. I regret nothing because without those moments in my life I would not be where I am today. The Universe does not make mistakes—this is something I live by and remind myself of every day. As women, we need to be clear about what we want, and strong enough to stand up and say "This is mine!" Own your life, and embrace that beautiful, strong power within you!

It Begins with Self

by Nichole Terry

Everywhere I look, I see a new self-help book that is springing up online, attempting to tell people advice about why they are single, miserable, and sexually frustrated. While all of these books are relatively helpful to those who may pick them up, they all seem to begin motivating people to put all of their efforts into transforming, changing, or "fixing" their mate rather than themselves. This misdirected focus only proceeds to increase the problems that people experience in relationships because it leads people to expect the dysfunctional egomaniac that they picked up at the grocery store to miraculously change a lifelong stream of recurring issues and failed relationships. They don't realize that conflicts with their temporarily significant other are a recurring issue that may be better addressed starting with themselves, and not with a random proclamation of how women and men each come from uninhabitable planets, or how to train your man like your golden retriever (which doesn't work—I've tried).

Oh, the recurring dramas of the romantic relationship, are they ever a positive thing? It is so hard to believe that with all of the divorces, cheating, and episodes of *"Who the 'bleep' Did I Marry?" and "Snapped,"* that people are even continuing to become involved with them at all. It would seem that humans are determined to find that one person who is going to explain away their lives, improve their piteous self-view, and reverse decades of their mother's criticism merely by popping up in their lives. The only reason that people crave romantic attention so much is that they swear that they will feel better about themselves, their existence, and their circumstances by having it. We are all just so positive that the adding of extra drama, baggage, and anxiety attacks over someone who can barely control their own lives is just what we need for self-improvement.

Unfortunately, this dependence on outer validation frequently results in eventual realizations that the person we invested so much of our time and money into has taken both of those things and run off with a much uglier and meaner version of ourselves.

And the cycle begins again—"Why the hell did this happen again? I thought I knew what I wanted!? I picked the wrong one again!? I made the same mistake again!? How am I supposed to fix this!? I thought I was fixing it! I'm not good enough again!? Was I ever good enough!? Will I ever be good enough!? What's wrong with me!?" When allowed, these feelings of anger and hopelessness, which result from a failed relationship, eventually begin grinding away at your soul. The rage that sits in your heart then proves toxic to your spirit and deteriorates you from the inside out. This can sometimes result in a total loss of self, which is then manifested through either violently breaking living room windows, or worse, an internalized pain that lasts for years to come. It's these unfortunate things that are symptoms of the internal, pre-existing issues we are really dealing with, and not the fact that you once again have carve out a budget for several online dating services because, heaven knows, you have to pay for all of them if you are eventually going to land that husband.

The problems that we have with those we love or form relationships with are the result of unresolved fears, lies, or issues that have become integral parts of our thought processes over the years. For example, the fact that I had remained heartbroken over one man for six years was not my problem. My problem was that I was angry I could not fix or change his feelings about me—I was angry that I could not fix or change his feelings about me because I felt that I had to convince him that I was good enough for him. I felt that I had to convince him that I was good enough for him because I chose to despise myself as a result of years of expressed disapproval from those around me, including family and friends. Accordingly, because I did not make the decision to feel good about myself and see myself worthy despite what others thought, I now formed a destructive and cyclical belief that I was worthless and not deserving of anyone's love, not even my own.

The truth is that our own love is the only love that we can guarantee ourselves. I'm not by any means saying that we should stop desiring companionship or wanting that seemingly impossible mate that only exists on the movie screen. Rather, I am saying that looking to this mate or companion for validation of self will fail every single time. If you have no love for yourself, even if this person is good to you and for you, you won't see it, appreciate it, or acknowledge it. A good mate should be the supplement to an already enjoyable, balanced, and self-fulfilling life. As long as we base our happiness on the success of our romantic relationships, we will never be happy.

The reality that others can't provide self-validation is reflected in our everyday dealings. The Universe will not respond to fear with positivity or to negativity with optimism. The Law of Attraction states that like attracts like. Therefore, if you enter a relationship with your mate full of fear and negativity, convinced that they cannot be trusted, and convinced that they will only abandon you to the loneliness and self-pity that you have known so many times before, then that must be what happens. They can only prove to you what you already believe.

The objective is to place your trust, dependence, and unconditional love in yourself. That is the only place these things can always be found. If you think that isn't true, then look around at the relationships in your life. How many times have you given another person the ability to put you out of your mind or make you lose focus? How many times have you left an interaction feeling negatively or unworthy? How many times have you clenched your teeth and fought back tears from the thought of the harsh words spoken by another person? You can blame them as much as possible, but that blame will not erase the fact that you allowed yourself to feel this way and therefore must now suffer in these miserable emotions by yourself while they move on from your life without a glance back in your direction.

So, how can you change this thought process of self-disapproval after years and years of self-rejection? Start small. There are several wonderful things about you. You don't think so? Well, you can read, you can see, you can process information, you can think critically and problem solve. You're reading this. Good start. Now, take it a little further: you can identify your negative thoughts and you can change them. This means you have power. Isn't it a relief that your control freak of a boss isn't the one forcing you into anxiety on a daily basis? This power is where it begins. This mere realization is enough to take you down the path of eventual self-acceptance and self-love because you are the one who can direct this journey and make the decision to bounce back when those negative, hurtful thoughts pop into your brain again and again.

The journey to reverse years of repeated self-abuse and battering is not going to end immediately, and it most likely will not be easy. However, when you feel like you cannot beat the recurring negatively that has dominated your life up to this point, try to focus on these next few positive thoughts: your very presence on this earth is a miracle. Your spirit emerged from a miraculous void to experience—enjoy and benefit from this existence. How you do these things is up to you. However, the very fact that you are an incredible manifestation of spiritual uniqueness is enough to justify the extensive journey towards loving and enjoying yourself. And when this love for self becomes a dominant part of your life, no one else will ever be able to change your feelings about "you," and then the cyclical nightmarish relationships and heartbreak will end for good.

Esther Hicks stated that, "[*we are] insecure because we never decided to be secure.*" Take this truth to heart and decide to be secure in yourself today. It's the only love that you can guarantee will be there every day, every hour, every minute and every second of your amazing life.

Leaping is Believing

by Erin Rose

When I think back to my life just one year ago today, it is almost unfathomable to me how much has changed since then. My life is so completely different than it was a mere 365 days ago, it is hard to believe that I am still even the same person. Last year, my life was more or less what you might call "status quo." I got up every day, did what I was supposed to do, got the bills paid, and made sure to have some fun when I could. I worked hard. I had a full time job. It was getting me by. It was killing me.

Mentally, emotionally, spiritually, physically—I could actually feel my life force diminishing. I was a social worker and I am here to tell you that the stories you hear about social workers are true. I was overworked, underpaid, overstressed, under-appreciated—check, check, check, and check. Every day was a whirlwind of appointments, meetings, paperwork, catastrophes, and crises. Just when I thought I was all caught up, more work would shuffle into place. Important work. Work that needed to be done. Now.

For just a little over a year, I was able to do my job and do it well with no serious, visible repercussions on my well-being. Then the cracks started to show. As my caseload got heavier and the expectations grew taller, my anxieties began to spike. One by one, the symptoms of my breaking spirit were rearing up and clinging so tightly to my being that removing them myself would have been like a fish trying to pull a hook out of its own mouth. I was losing sleep. Awake half the night, I'd be worrying about either a child (or two) or the mountain of paperwork I needed to catch up on the next day. I started having chest pains so fearsome it was difficult to stand up straight. Sometimes I would get a twinge of pain in my heart so piercing it would take my breath away. I developed an eye twitch. My menstrual cycle was down to just 19 days. I gained weight. My relationship was suffering.

So what did I do? I did what any honest-to-goodness, blue-blooded American would do in the same situation: I got medicated. I went to my doctor to verify that I was not indeed, dying a slow and absurd death-by-fretfulness. Then we got down to the business of essentially tossing mini-marshmallows at the immoveable mountain resting squarely on my psyche. We reduced the anxiety medication I was already on and added a new one. Then we increased the dose of the second one. When that didn't work, we scrapped the first two medications and tried a brand new one altogether. Then we increased the dose. Then we threw the second one back into the mix, and increased that dosage. Then, to top it all off, like a cherry on some sort of perverse chemical sundae, we added a benzo (Klonopine) to be taken "as needed, in case of panic."

What the what!? Why on Earth was I putting myself through all of this just to do a job I was barely tolerating? Simply put, I didn't think I had any other choice. I had bills to pay, I needed health insurance, and my Bachelors in psychology didn't seem to qualify me for much else. I felt boxed in, cornered, as if I had spent a lifetime working and developing skills that I no longer had any interest in using. Looking back, it's safe to say that I was quite terrified. I knew things couldn't go on that way forever, but I couldn't see any viable way out. I was blinded by duty and crippled by fear. Yet, I knew I was on a collision course—my life frenzying to a fever pitch that was ultimately going to crash and burn, leaving me nothing but a pile of ash.

How did I get myself to this point in the first place? I would dare argue that it happened in the most usual way. Up until that point, there were certain facts about my life that I had long ago just accepted as "truth." For one, I had never figured out what I wanted in life. I knew I had dreams and passions, but they were elusive. I couldn't quite put my finger on them or give them a name. Certainly, they were not tangible enough to build a living on. So, I let them go. I put them on the back burner and shifted my energy to getting by in life. At the time, this seemed like the right thing to do—a girl's got to eat right? Two additional "truths" I had always maintained for myself were:

1. I would NEVER go back to school (I hated college) and
2. I would never EVER move back to my home town in Vermont (I hate winter).
I was certain. Period. I believed them to be requirements for my ultimate happiness, so they were unequivocally non-negotiable.

Then the most ridiculous thing happened. I crashed. It didn't come with the super-sonic boom of destruction that I had been expecting it to, but it did come, just as I knew it would. Oddly enough, the explosion was a gentle one, more like a baby chick breaking out of its shell than a bomb detonating. And when I looked up to see the aftermath, it wasn't ash I felt raining down upon my face, it was glitter.

I realized it wasn't really an explosion at all. It was an epiphany. I haven't had a lot of first hand or even second hand experience with epiphany, so it took me a minute to catch on. Epiphanies are tricky. When you aren't paying attention they creep into all the little pieces of your life and flip them on their heads. Then when you look back again, something that was once familiar and mundane is now foreign and brand new. It was like epiphany came over to the house of my psyche, tossed everything up in the air, and called "heads or tails!" Some things landed as they had always had been, and some touched ground again as their perfect opposite.

Just like that, the choices were clear. I don't use the

phrase 'just like that' lightly, but it really did happen that way. Suddenly, where once were questions so terrifying I couldn't even broach them, there were now only answers. All of the 'never could's turned into 'why not's? With an unheard of clarity, I understood that I needed to let go of my faltering relationship. Within two weeks, I turned in my notice at work. I gave my energy back to my dreams and started researching schools. And, insanity of insanities, moving home to Vermont suddenly became the thing to do.

Now, it was a radical change. It was like I really did wake up one day and everything that I had always known and believed no longer applied. The 'answers' seemed to go against my every notion of what I needed to be happy in life. This is what makes epiphanies so tricky. While the clarity of conviction had arrived, it was still something I had to choose. The universe had shown me the prospect of a life I could be living, and if I wanted it I was going to have to leap.

In the end, leaping was easy. I simply could not carry on as I was. If the universe was kind enough to present me with the path to my dreams, who was I to turn it away because I had misgivings about some of the side roads? So I chose to leap— and believe. Believing is really the important part—trusting that the risks you are taking are worthwhile no matter the outcome. But, truly, the two go hand in hand. Leaping implies believing. Once the choice was made, fear was automatically replaced by faith.

That was nine months ago. Today, I am living in Vermont, enrolled in school, trained as a holistic life coach, and well on my way to achieving the life of my dreams. What's more, I sleep like a dream, my chest pains and eye twitches are a thing of the past, I am losing weight, and the very best part: I am 100% medication free! This is not to say that there aren't challenges. I still hate winter. I'm still not that fond of school. I definitely miss the steady paycheck and the life I had in Nashville. I often experience fear that perhaps I won't be able to see this whole thing through.

But, here is the big difference. A year ago, I literally felt my life closing in around me. No matter which direction I turned, I could feel the walls inching in, and I too was shrinking to fit inside that tightening space. Today, my life is ever expanding. The walls have been blasted away from the inside out, and when I gaze around, I see infinite possibilities. I stand in the middle, radiating passion, and joy, and excitement for what's to come. Sure there are tough days, and I get frustrated, but this only the beginning. Even on days when that old fear comes creeping in, I stand tall—proud of myself for leaping and grateful for the gift of believing.

Life Lessons

by Donna Gosselin

I have discovered that being in my fifties now allows me to look back on my life and learn from experiences over the course of my life. I grew up in an average, middle-class family during the 1970's—working dad, stay-at-home mom, two kids, and a dog. I had a great childhood, and with the exception of the usual angst, I can't really complain too much about my teenage years either.

I entered the adult world in the 1980's. My generation, myself included, fell into the cult of the individual. I was self centered, focused on making money, and convinced I was going to take the world by storm. I met a guy who was just as self-absorbed. By the early 90's, we were married and raising two children. Life still seemed pretty good and, over time, I began to change as a person. The primary focus of my life was no longer me, but the two small people that I was responsible for.

Nothing changes your life more than having children. Your entire set of priorities change. I was following in the footsteps of my mother by being a stay-at-home mom, and this was also the time where I began my spiritual awakening. Now, when I say spiritual awakening, I'm basically taking about feeling the presence of a higher power in my life that I was never really taught to understand when I was younger.

That spiritual presence made itself known on one night in particular. My nine-year old son and I were on top of his bunk-bed hanging posters. My six-year old daughter was playing on the bottom bunk. Suddenly, I heard this very audible voice in my head say, "tell her to get off the bed." So I did. As soon as she got off the bottom bunk, the entire bed collapsed with my son and I on top of it. All I could think at the time was that she would have been crushed under the weight of the bed frame, the upper mattress, and the two of us.

But, it was the events of September 11, 2001 that not only changed the world, but also began changes in my own life that I never expected. I turned forty that day—the dreaded beginning of middle age, and I remember waking up depressed and trying to tell myself that I would not let turning forty bother me. After watching the horrors of that day unfold, it put my entire life in a different perspective. Getting older no longer bothered me. I welcomed growing older and wiser, and that spiritual presence in my life became stronger, even if I really didn't understand what it was trying to tell me.

My forties also opened up a completely new chapter of my life. My husband of sixteen years left me to raise two children alone, stating that he needed to find himself because he didn't have the life he wanted. I found myself with no job, a house we couldn't afford, and two children to raise. Anytime the spiritual presence felt like giving me some advice, I was open to suggestions. But things always managed to work out. I found a job, the house was sold, and I was on my way to being just fine. I'd like to say that we had no hardships, but if I did, I'd be lying. We had a lot of hardships. I bought a new house, I lost my job, and subsequently lost the new house. I began dating an old friend and went through some rough times with not only my own kids, but his kids too. Still, that spiritual presence kept telling me that everything was going to be fine, I believed it, and trudged on.

Now the kids are grown and out on their own. I have built a new life, but something was still not quite right. I was working as a crisis intake interviewer and knew that this was not the career for me. I loved the idea of helping people through life's bumps in the road—and Lord knows I've had my fair share of bumps—but because of the nature of my job, I was unable to help people the way I wanted.

That's when I had another experience with the spiritual presence that occasionally likes to make itself known. I was having an especially bad day at work and went to buy my lunch, which was out of the ordinary. I always brought lunch from home. I was in a restaurant waiting for my lunch order when a man came up to me and put his hand on my shoulder. He said, "I hope you don't think I'm invading your privacy, but I just wanted to let you know that a lot of people are praying for you and things will be okay." I didn't know what to say except, "thank you, I appreciate that." I watched the man go back to his table where he was sitting with an elderly gentleman who smiled at me. Shortly after that, my order was brought out and when I stood up to say goodbye to the men, their table was empty with no sign that anyone was just there. They couldn't have left because I was sitting right next to the door, so I would have seen them leave. I looked around the restaurant and no one fitting their description was there. I drove back to work slightly baffled and a little freaked out, but I knew everything was going to be alright. That afternoon at work was much better than the morning was.

A few months later, I was shopping with my daughter at an upscale grocery store one day and stumbled across an article in a free magazine about the Radiant Health Institute and their life coach training. It was like being slapped in the head with a two-by-four. This was it! This was what I was looking for! But, of course, second thoughts kicked in, like, "will I be good at this? Can I really help people? What if I guide someone in the wrong direction?" My daughter was my biggest cheerleader. She told me to go for it. My significant other told me to go for it. And that nagging spiritual presence in my life told me, "you will regret it if you don't do it." So I did, and I'm a new person.

Now I am a certified holistic life coach, and some of my friends still don't understand what it is that I do, but that's okay. Through my training, I have discovered an inner peace. I've learned to look at issues in my life more objectively and make the right decisions for me. Even though I am still working at the drug rehabilitation crisis intake, the job no longer stresses me the way it used to. I sleep better. My eating habits have changed, I exercise more, and my health has improved greatly. And that spiritual presence? It's there stronger than ever now, and it's always letting me know that everything is going to work out.

I've learned to trust what the spiritual presence tells me because I know it won't steer me wrong. Is it my guardian angel? I don't know, but I would like to believe it is. But, whatever it is, it has led me to this point where I am living a truly blessed and radiant life.

Mental-Emotional Health Matters

by Megan Johnson Rox

Your spirit, higher self, inner genius, God, all-that-is, or whatever you want to call it speaks to you often through emotions. It's important to pay attention to what you're feeling.

I've been experiencing a lot of stress, anxiety, and fatigue these past couple of months and because I'm closely connected with my spirit, I know it's because I didn't listen to my divine guidance that was telling me I should not take on six classes this semester. From years of past experience, I have become aware of that restless, anxious feeling that comes when I am not following the path I'm meant to and am not listening to my inner, spiritual guidance. With teaching six classes, I'm too busy to devote enough time to the things that I really want to do (and am meant to do): making music and teaching or publicly speaking on personal and spiritual development. My spirit tried to tell me this several months ago, but I didn't listen, so it's now trying to tell me by hitting me upside the head with a 2x4. This is a way your spirit tries to talk to you (see Mona Lisa Shultz's book, Awakening Intuition, for a great example of spirit trying to talk to you and the gradually severe consequences of not listening).

My quest to help and teach others what I've learned to help life be so much better has proven to be helpful during my dark periods when I succumb to ego. The reason I haven't been able to manage my stress lately is that I haven't been meditating regularly. I've been too busy, tired and I had lots of lame excuses for why I haven't, but I know it's so crucial! Of course there's a reason for everything, and I wouldn't have felt compelled to talk about stress and anxiety management in relation to spirit-ego if I hadn't experienced it myself recently. I'm thankful to still be close enough to my spirit that I don't feel completely controlled by my ego and can catch glimpses of my experience from a broader, outside perspective.

No negative emotion is good to experience for an extended period of time. The only exception I can think of might be grief. Negative emotions such as stress and anxiety are the kind of emotions that are prevalent in our society today, and are not good to feel for an extended period of time.

I know many people say it's good to feel emotions of any kind, and that we shouldn't be afraid of them, try to avoid feeling them, or push them down or away. I believe this is beneficial, but only if you have the goal of acknowledging, working through, and releasing the emotion.

You're not meant to feel negative, fear or ego-based emotions for extended periods of time. However, it's hard to work through an emotion if you're living from ego. This is why you should strive to be connected with your spirit on a daily basis. When I'm doing this, I can use healthy strategies, such as energy work and spiritual exercises like meditation, to work through negative emotions. Some people get caught up trying to analyze why they're feeling this emotion. That's not the best way to go because we can't always know the reason behind the emotion. I argue it doesn't necessarily matter—as long as we just release it and move on, especially if the negative, pent up emotion stems from a traumatic experience.

As Deborah King, master healer, teacher, and author, says, it's not necessary to re-live certain old traumas in order to release the emotions and blocks that they may be causing you. You often don't get clarity on the causes of the negative emotion while you are feeling it because, when you're overwhelmed with a negative emotion, you're not in spirit, you're in ego. Remember, spirit is pure love.

When you release the negative emotion, you are

one with spirit again and you'll be surprised at the clarity that comes. You'll probably even realize the causes of your negative emotions at this point.

The grass really is always greener on the "other side." I've been surprised at how much clarity I get about my life from an outside perspective when I'm connected with my spirit. It's because I really am viewing my life from a different perspective—that of truth.

Our egos create an illusion of our "reality" based on separateness and limitations. When we realize we are all connected, abundance and love is limitless. We can create our own reality. We realize we are powerful beyond measure. The only things that get in our way sometimes, because we're human, are our ego and fear.

Any negative emotion can be linked to fear. Once you realize fear is the only thing getting in the way of your connection with spirit, and therefore your ability to feel love and have abundance, you will realize that allowing this emotion to take over is not a good thing. You have the power to overcome your ego. Too many people accept feeling mentally and emotionally crappy for extended periods of time. This should not be acceptable.

If you find yourself feeling very stressed, anxious, or any other negative emotional state for an extended period of time, you need to do something to change your attitude or your environment. Granted, time is relative, so only you can tap into your intuition and feel what is too long for you. For me, it's longer than a month. When I feel stressed for longer than a month, I know it's something deeper than the occasional, situational stress that comes and goes.

Stress is very common and is frequently the kind of thing that, when prolonged, can cause people to feel like they need to drink, smoke, or use another negative coping strategy when they get home from work. I noticed this pattern in myself over the past couple of months. In addition to needing a drink or smoke when I got home from school, I noticed the stress was causing me to be unusually fatigued. That led to not feeling like cooking healthy meals every night, which led to me feeling even worse, which made me want to drink and smoke more, which made me more stressed. It became a viscous cycle.

Too many people who are in a similar cycle don't recognize it or do anything about it. It can easily lead to depression. I know this from experience. Many people go to a psychiatrist to get psychiatric drugs for relief, thinking there must be something wrong with their minds. Let me tell you, from experience, this does not help—it only makes things worse because the reason you were probably feeling crappy to begin with is that you weren't following your intuition. You need to be honest with yourself and always be true to your unique desires and talents. You should strive for a happy or, at least, peaceful existence.

Why would you want to settle for anything less?

It's very empowering when you no longer feel controlled by your ego's whims and instead are in control. Strive to let your spirit "take the driver's seat" in your life.

My Journey to Radiant Living

by Jazzy Sdlihc

Close your eyes and think about the meaning of Radiant Living. Can you imagine what a radiant life looks like? See if you can feel what it may feel like. The images and feelings may vary depending on the person, but one thing is certain; we all are capable of having radiant lives. It took me almost my entire life to realize that I had this bright light on the inside waiting for me to let it shine. I want to take you on my journey, my path, my mission which ultimately led to my Radiant Living.

As a child, I was always the go-to person for advice, comfort, counsel, or just an ear to listen. I had no idea that I was simply preparing myself for my destiny. Though I was being an aide to others, I needed my own self-healing. I was very timid and afraid on the inside, which often was reflected on the outside. In a sense, I was depriving myself of happiness. I was too shy to speak up for myself and too fearful to do the things that I really wanted to do. My self-esteem was not my ally. I allowed myself to be overlooked and taken advantage of by friends and family. I doubted my abilities. I sheltered my gifts. I eventually settled for things and people that I didn't need in my life.

Now, when I say settled, I mean I accepted being treated in a way that I knew I didn't deserve. So what did I deserve? I deserved happiness and fulfillment, not anger and depression. How could I allow myself to be in an abusive relationship? I often asked myself this question. I didn't come from a broken home where my father was absent or abusive. At that time, my parents were going on forty years of marriage. Something just wasn't adding up. I eventually solved my own problem. I had unknowingly subtracted God out of the equation. When I realized my error, I began to correct it whole-heartedly. Going through and surviving an abusive relationship has made me a stronger person. I had no idea that this would be my first stepping stone to Radiant Living.

The next step I took was huge! To an outsider, it would appear to be a catastrophic event, but in all actuality, it was a definite life changer. In April of 2005, my mind, body, and soul had decided that they couldn't take any more stress. The relief of ending my abusive relationship was a great feeling. I was no longer being physically or emotionally abused, but it wasn't a complete success because I was still carrying around unresolved issues. Within three long, terrifying days, I had become paralyzed from the points of my shoulders to the tips of my toes and everything in between. After two days of neurological testing, I was told that I have what's called Gullian Barré Syndrome (GBS). This is a very rare disorder that affects 1 person out of every 100,000. In the same sentence, I was told that it would be a year until I would be able to move again. I believed, for a split moment, that time stood still and I was simply dreaming. Those thoughts diminished in a split second and I had to accept that this was my current reality.

Needless to say, it was an eye-opening reality. I spent one month in ICU at a medical hospital, one month at a nursing home, and one month at a physical rehabilitation hospital. By the way, I proved the doctors wrong; the previous one-year prognosis ended at three months. Transitioning to each place made me appreciate every single thing about life. My faith increased and humility became my middle name. I accepted the pain, the struggle, and the challenge of my condition. I had to learn how to walk again, feed myself again, and go the bathroom without wearing diaper. I knew that I was on a road to recovery physically and mentally. My life, friends, and family meant much more to me than stress. I began to become more verbal in expressing my feelings. I even learned how to tell someone, "No!" This sparked a flame in me to want to live my life better. But, this was not the end of my journey, it was just the beginning!

I went through minor struggles in my recovery process. Other than the obvious physical recovery, I had to change my lifestyle. My kids and I had to move to my parents' house. I had to finish six months of outpatient rehab before I could resume working. When I finally did, it was only for three hours a day. I literally had to "process the process". After a year, I was back to working full time and had my own home again, but still had pieces of depression holding on to me. Something was still missing. I'd survived two undeniably life-changing events, but wasn't really feeling happier or fulfilled. The flame was lit, but I had to discover what could keep it going. From that point, I began searching for my purpose and what I really enjoyed doing.

I had realized my true passion. I believed that I was put on this Earth to guide, encourage, and heal those that are in need. I thought back to when I was a child doing these things for friends and family. After all the years, I was still passionate about it. I then decided to go back to college and get a degree in Social Work. Going back to school had empowered me more than I ever imagined. I was now surrounding myself with positive people who were focused on the same goal as mine. In 2008, I graduated with a degree in Social Work. After graduation, I never worked a single job in my field. A career in Social Work just didn't seem to fit my character or personality. I desired to share my compassion and spirit freely without being confined to a desk or cubicle. At this time, another childhood passion that I had tightly tucked away resurfaced.

In fall of 2009, for the first time in my shy, fearful life, I performed my own personal poetry in front of an audience. The crowd was taken away by my lyrical content and powerful inspiration. It completely shocked me to find that I had this much impact on that many people. Needless to say, my confidence and energy level went through the roof! I began to record my poems and sell them on

CD. My flame was no doubt burning with full force. I was finally placing the pieces of my puzzle together. My words that have always helped, healed, and provided comfort; it just took me a while to acknowledge that my past was just the pre-game show and this was the first kick off.

I knew that if I was able to overcome fears and began exploring my gifts, I would be able to unlock the door to happiness. So, I continued my journey of self-discovery. All these great ideas began to pop up in my mind. I used my writing as a tool to empower people around me and those that I had never met. The more I let go of doubts, fears, and insecurities, the more I was able to be free. Freedom is the major attribute necessary to live a radiant life.

The map to freedom lies within you! Although I went through highs and lows, I was still able to find fulfillment. But only, and I mean only, could I have done it once I let go of the lows and saw what remained. Naturally, we're not the exactly the same and our stories will differ, but the beauty of it all is that we still have the same purpose in life. Simply put, our purpose is to be happy, loved, and fulfilled. These blessings we must share with each other.

I believe in making sure that all parts of our being are secure. We are made up of the mind, body, and spirit. In order to keep ourselves whole, we must be in sync with these three facets. I am all about empowering, strengthening, and promoting balance to maintain happiness within one self. I encourage you to have freedom of mind, body, and soul. You must take all factors of your being into account. "You" have to be held accountable for your feelings, thoughts, and actions. We all must embrace lessons on this journey that we call Life! And when we do, we no longer image what Radiant Living looks like; we only feel it.

Radiant Life

by Michelle Jones

Living a Radiant Life is simply a mere matter of perception. Have you ever heard of the saying, "The glass is half empty or full," when it has exactly the same amount of water in it in both instances? The same can apply to life. Whether you view life as half empty or half full is essentially your perception of life. The beautiful thing about perception is that it is a choice. You have the ability to choose if the glass is half empty or half full. Which one are you currently choosing? Some of us, though do not realize it, are stuck in the position of a half-empty life. Some of us unfortunately live in this half-empty state for years. One of the reasons we do not realize that we are stuck in this state of life is because we lack awareness of our state of being. Until we free ourselves of this unconscious living, we will never be able to live a radiant life.

Choosing to view life as a full glass of radiance depends on your present state of awareness. Awareness is defined as, "the state or condition of being aware; having knowledge; consciousness." Reading this book at this very moment is bringing to your awareness the choice you have to change your perception of your life. Life mentors are wonderful resources to heighten your awareness. Mentors come in a variety of fashions. They can come in the form of a friend, teacher, co-worker or even an author of a book. You may even resonate with someone who is famous. You may find that their words inspire you to explore topics that raise your awareness. Find someone you look up to or someone you are drawn to on a spiritual level. Chances are you already have that person around you and your awareness will guide you to them. One way to bring this person into awareness is to think about your relationship with that person. Do you tend to go to that person every time you have a problem? Is that person always supportive of your efforts? Does this person guide you to the positive when you're choosing to view the negative? It's normal to have several people who help you to raise your awareness throughout your life time.

As you change and become more conscious, the people around you will change. You will notice that people who surround you have your best interest in mind. Try not to be judgmental of this process. Surrounding yourself with people who facilitate growth is neither good nor bad—it just is. Simply being around that person will tell you things about yourself that you never realized before. These things have always been there but you were not aware of them. Certain talents you had not considered may "arise" into your awareness when, for instance, a friend thinks you're the best at something. That friend brought that skill or talent to your awareness. Once you become aware of it, it's likely that you will make different choices that highlight your "new" talent. Have you seen the video on the internet where women were asked to describe themselves to a forensic artist? The forensic artist sat behind a wall and never physically laid eyes on the women. He was then asked to sketch a portrait of them as they described their features in detail. One beautiful woman, who had gorgeous eyes, described her eyes as clearly not as attractive as they truly were. This was her truth, but not true in reality. Another person was asked to describe the same women after becoming familiar with her. The sketch that was made from woman's description of herself was far less attractive than the sketch produced from the stranger's description. Every single one of the women who described themselves ended up with a sketch which looked sad or unflattering. Had this experiment not happened, these women wouldn't have been aware of how they saw themselves versus how others viewed them. That moment could be described as a moment of clarity or moment of awareness. Being aware of your right to choose in life is a very powerful tool that you can use to create a more radiant life, not only for you, but for those around you.

Once you have become aware of the ability to make choices, you then are able to learn how the choices you make are determined. You will begin to silently reflect and ask yourself, "I wonder why I choose to do that?" The way you choose to view life is impacted by life experiences. If you had a mother, for example, who always scolded you every time you made what you considered to be the best choice, you will not feel confident in your ability to make choices. Not feeling confident in your ability to choose can lead you down the path of choosing the path of most resistance, which in turn can lead you down a very difficult life. A lot of us spend a lot of time on a path that is resisting us because of not being aware of how our choices are impacting our lives.

Our friends and family also impact our choices. It's easy to fall into choosing what everyone else is choosing. A lot of times we are not even conscious we are doing it! Have you ever had the friend that talked you into going out to eat when you really weren't hungry to begin with? In the back of your mind, your thoughts quickly ran through all the things you set your mind to doing that evening that did not involve going out to eat. That very moment is when you made the decision to go out to eat, despite the uneasy feeling it left in your body. This choice was impacted by someone else's choice! Imagine the other areas in our lives where we "jump on the band wagon" of choices! How did choosing to go out to eat feel when you didn't really want to go in the first place? To some, it could feel like you have wasted two hours of your life and felt unproductive. Others would think of what they "should have" done instead of doing what someone else wanted them to do, which could result in anger. The positive thing about that situation is that it brings to your awareness your ability to choose differently. Next time, you will remember what it felt like to do something you didn't want to do and in that moment you will decide to choose otherwise. This moment of clarity is very powerful, and you should give yourself great credit for accomplishing it and noticing! This means you have heightened your awareness, which clears the path for different choices in the future and allows your life to flow like a river of beautiful radiance! Giving in to other people's choices that are made for you is giving your power away to them. This is in no way fulfilling to your own life path. We are here to master our lives and find our path to happiness, not give in to everyone else's needs and desires if they are not in line with our own. When you are conscious of your choices, you are taking your power back. Congratulations! It feels great to claim and own your power! The more you own the power within yourself, the more apt you are to helping those around you without steering away from your own path. Please don't think of this as selfish. Have you heard of the expression in terms to airline safety, "put your own oxygen mask on first?"

The same method could be applied to life. If you don't put your own oxygen mask on and take care of your needs first, how can you be available to help others? Could you imagine what the world would be like if everyone was completely in line with their life's path and helped everyone else out along the way? It would be heaven on earth!

Choosing to perceive life as a radiant, beautiful gift full of joy, love, and abundance is entirely up to you. How you chose to perceive life is impacted by your present state of awareness. Your current level of awareness is impacted by the company you keep, your life experiences, and mentors who have been present along your path in life. This process is a miraculously beautiful thing because no matter where you are in your life, no matter what stage in your life you're at, no matter how old you are, you can choose to change your perception at any moment! When your perception of life changes, your life changes! This is what it means to live a life full of radiance and beauty!

Sister Circles: Villages of Sisterhood

by Ashiya L. Swan

The ability to connect with another human being and build a meaningful relationship is foundational to meeting our basic needs as human beings. This need for connection does not arise from ego or the lack thereof. When we engage any relationship, we move beyond those things that separate us to create the balance and harmony of unity. Building reciprocity with another person is a divine act beyond human faculties, rooted in the essence of our Spirit. Many of the challenges we face in life occur because we lose sight of the fact that God is omnipresent. When the presence of our loved ones brings us joy, we find ourselves in the presence of God, even if it is not understood. Our relationships become sacred as we mimic our need to for connection with our Creator. These sacred circles are extensions of relationship with God because we are given the chance to radiate and reflect the love, beauty, and joy God offers us in each moment.

"It takes a village to raise a child." African Proverb

Our earliest relationships gift us with the ability to build and sustain personal, romantic, and professional relationships as we move into adulthood. The connections we build with our parents or those who care for us are our most obvious examples as children. Viewing our childhood as a whole, we are just as often influenced by our siblings, extended family, and those people most important to our caregivers. Through family, friendships, and extended circles, our village naturally forms around us. They provide us with the instruction, guidance, and love necessary for our growth. Without labeling the experience of our village as good or bad, we can see these relationships increase in value as we navigate life armed with the lessons of our youth.

"If you want to go fast, go alone. If you want to go

far, go together." African Proverb

For adult women, our villages often grow to include a circle of women bound by shared life experiences. By devoting love and understanding to these friendships from the same place that we offer love to our mothers, aunts, and sisters, we create our Sister Circle. As an extension of our village that corrected us as young girls, our Sister Circles serve as a source of inspiration and motivation to us as women. The collective generational wisdom of our mothers, grandmothers, and aunts is the strength of the Sister Circle. Borrowing wisdom from diverse viewpoints helps us expand our perception and options in life. Each friendship represents a wealth of wisdom otherwise unavailable to us. By offering the best of what we received from our village to our circles, we expand to meet current times and create a new level of understanding.

Life Lessons Reflected

As friendships blossom, we find ourselves connecting with different members of our circle depending on our needs at the moment. If we look closely, we may see our closest friends bring the same balance to our lives as members of our village. Whether conscious or not, our ability to recognize and rely on the right person could offer us the exact perspective we need at the right time. Where our villages instruct us, our Sister Circles reflect on those lessons and teach them when necessary. Authentic friendships thrive on the lessons of life. Authenticity encourages honesty and sincerity among friends that sets the stage for correction without malice. A genuine connection creates a real desire to see our friends live at their best. When we share hard truths with love and compassion, our Sister Circles are strengthened through our commitment to helping each other develop our highest potential.

Guidance and Accountability

Deciding the type of woman one will become in a world with overwhelming suggestions is a hard task for any young woman. Despite the endless sources of suggestions, much of who we are is shaped by the women in our villages. The women that raised us represented a standard as we unknowingly decided what was "different" or "acceptable" based on who they were. Their presence was a prototype that influenced how we made decisions and grew as women. Honoring the vision we develop of ourselves as women is the foundation of the bonds that form Sister Circles. Regardless of the nature of images from our village and society, they influence us as we decide who we are and who we are not. As we continue to determine who we are for ourselves, our friends are there to hold us accountable. In developing our sense of self, our need for guidance becomes a desire for honesty from someone we know intimately. Instead of telling us who we should be, our friends remind us of who we've decided we want to be.

Role Models of Inspiration

Observing the choices and subsequent consequences of the women in our lives as children creates a window through which we view the world. Their choices laid the groundwork for what we deem acceptable in life. Whether we subscribe to their beliefs or not, our mothers, grandmothers, sisters, and any women close to our childhood have given us a view of how life could be. Quite naturally, we held fast to those things that caused us to thrive and shunned what did not. As we mature, our role models and examples of womanhood are reflected in the lives of those we associate with most. As we work toward our own goals and dreams, our friends inspire by manifesting their own dreams. Our circles inspire us to want more for ourselves than we thought possible and affirm our belief in ourselves and our abilities.

Unconditional Love and Confidence

At some point in our development, we are sure to meet a woman that allows us the space to be authentic and real. We are able to question life through their eyes without experiencing any judgment or ridicule. In this space, we develop and reveal our true nature. When we find a moment free from the views of others, we welcome the risk of discovering our own. With someone there to guide us and love us, regardless of what we choose in life, we find comfort with what is foreign or unknown to us. Through their love, we mature in our ability to make decisions for ourselves. With time and trust, our Sister Circles become more sacred. While many of our needs change as we become women, there are some that will always remain the same. As we learn to process and respond to unexpected or challenging events in life, we still need a place of respite and refuge to think and reflect. The best friends offer us a sacred space to work through those moments by simply being present. They offer us the freedom to explore our feelings and our options without offering us unsolicited advice. Their love and guidance always guides us back to ourselves and helps us reflect our truth when requested.

Sacred Sisterhood

The gift of connection through friendship is a cornerstone of life for many women. In our most cherished relationships, we flow between sharing our gifts and preserving our needs. Fostering a connection with someone who understands where we are and where we have been is necessary self-care. These relationships provide us with someone who can see our unique position in life and be there with us when we need to find our balance. Our sacred sisterhoods are keep us fully engaged in a circle of radiant living.

Self-Confidence and Inner Strength

by Camila Velasco

When we begin to think about the truth of life and how important it is to be truthful, no one realizes what builds within ourselves. This is called confidence.

Confidence is not only believing that others are not going to fail us, it is also the fulfilling promises we make to ourselves.

For example, I always say to myself, "This will be the last hamburger this week because tomorrow I should start my diet" and the very next day will be the same. We will never fulfill what we say and our confidence will decrease. So, how can we talk about trusting others when we cannot keep our word with ourselves?

Why it is so important to restore confidence in yourself? It's because believing in yourself makes you feel more confident about you and makes you respect and be confident about others.

Confident people tend to make friends more easily. They communicate with respect to the needs of others and their own needs. They are usually good for resolving conflicts and disagreements. Abiding people are respected, so they know that their thoughts and feelings are important. They have confidence.

FACTORS THAT REDUCE CONFIDENCE

There are many factors in our life that reduce confidence. For example, the things we were hearing our parents and teachers say when we were kids like, "You're a fool" or "You can learn anything" or "You don't do anything right."

When we worry too much about pleasing others or worry if others do not agree or reject our ideas or opinions or feel sensitive to criticism or are hurt by past experiences in when our ideas were ignored or rejected, we do not develop the skills to become self-confident.

Confidence is an attitude towards life and can lead you to a very important decision – to become the victim or the protagonist.

Self-confidence is an attitude that allows individuals to have positive vision about themselves.

People who trust in themselves have realistic expectations. Even when their interests are not met, they continue to be positive and accept that way of being.

People with low self-confidence are overly dependent on the approval of others to feel good about themselves and to be valuable to others. Often those people who do not trust themselves do silly things to please others.

Improve your sense of humor and laugh and learn from your mistakes so you'll be more tolerant to failure.

Do things with patience, without fear of making mistakes. Failing is part of human nature.

Change negative thoughts about yourself. Speak to yourself with grace, love and respect.

Focus on how you feel about your behavior, work, etc. This will give you a stronger sense of yourself, avoiding always relying on what others think. Meditate, analyze and study who you are, where you want to go and how you want to be the best version of yourself.

Compare your Facebook photo with a real one. Take another photo of yourself look for the similarities.

Take risks and see new challenges as opportunities for growth instead of seeing them in terms of winning or losing. This opens up new possibilities and can increase your sense of acceptance of yourself.

Surround yourself with people who are nontoxic - with those that you think can teach you something - people who do not take your energy away but rather help you grow.

Do not compare yourself with others. Establish realistic challenges and goals for your life and do everything to achieve them.

Defeat your fear of speaking in public, not only in a class or a workshop, but in everyday life. Don't be afraid to give your opinion as it is very valuable.

We have a true fear is of being ridiculed so why not try to do something ridiculous in your life - something unimportant and laugh at yourself.

Strive to talk more with people on the subway, on the streets, etc. Talk to everyone. It helps you gain confidence and increases usually your level of culture.

It is not easy to understand, but when you are shy, most people think that you are strange even though you are normal. You can be a person who knows how to enjoy life and have good sense of humor.

For this reason, you have to improve your self-confidence and your self-esteem. Our greatest enemy is ourselves. Our minds are constantly saying negative things like, "I can't" or "I'll never achieve anything better."

Your way of thinking leads to some form of feeling that translates into a way of acting. Your internal representation determines your behaviors.

Many times a day we try to share with others, but

the frustration we feel with ourselves limits the progress of any kind of relationship with others. At that moment our energy becomes negative.

It is good to be patient and move forward slowly because if you want to improve overnight, you will become frustrated and will want to give up.

What is self-esteem? What is it for? It is the love and the value that we have for ourselves.

One of the keys to improving our self-esteem is to know to enjoy the present moment without thinking that something awaits us in the future. It is to be in this moment, here and now. By taking a cup of tea, taking a shower, watching a beautiful landscape, sipping a glass of wine, smiling at a child, and listening to the stories of elder people.

But this is an art and requires practice. Enjoying the positive and believing that any obstacle can be resolved are the main opportunities for improvement.

What is the biggest difference between having positive self-esteem and being selfish?

Self-esteem is the perception we have of ourselves, covering all aspects from the physical to the interior. The assessment takes place constantly and it does not always match reality. This is formed throughout our entire lives.

Love thy neighbor as thyself. Instead, the selfish person lacks love itself. In fact, selfishness is nothing more than a desperate attempt to hide the lack of love for oneself. The selfish person pretends to others and to yourself that you like yourself. This means that whoever does not love himself cannot love their neighbor.

Why is it necessary to have high self-esteem?

If we have a good appreciation of ourselves, we feel competent to overcome any challenge in our lives. It is necessary for the development of social skills.

Selfish people do not love other people or themselves. But if people loves themselves, then giving, helping and sharing all flow effortlessly. Moments of solitude are great for looking for something more in life like something we like to do - sitting alone, having breakfast and establishing very clear goals and dates.

Some tips for improving your self-esteem:

- Listen carefully to the inner positive voice; Make a list of things you do well, your talents or skills and your best qualities. Listen for, "I'm friendly" and "I am good with numbers" and "I cook very well."

- Determine new goals and objectives. Pursue your dreams.

- Visualize the goal you want to achieve even in the smallest detail. See yourself acting as reaching what you want or that you dream about. The image should be as clear as a color.

- Every morning upon awakening and every night before bed, watch the movie in your mind with pride, joy and satisfaction. Feel the emotions that this will cause in yourself. You accept that reality has many nuances. It all depends from where you look. Test it: look around you. Note everything you see and what angle you observe. Now sit on the floor and look at the same picture. Try to see things positively. What looks different?

- Practice, "Thank You." Every morning upon waking up, thank God, life or the universe for things that enrich your life or happiness. Name at least five blessings.

- Do this for 21 days straight since it will make your mind focus more on the positive.

- Do not forget that no one is born knowing how to do things. Everything requires practice and effort. We are all unique beings and blessed by God.

Paradoxically Whole

by Gina Manskar

A paradox is an apparent contradiction. It is something, such as a statement or situation, made up of two opposites that, at first glance, seem impossible but after some consideration do make sense. It seems that as we grow and change and our world view expands, we are presented with the challenge of holding two opposites in tension with each other. We can be pretty sure that when we begin to see things as paradoxical, we are in a growing season.

Exploring paradox can be both fascinating and challenging. I have come to value the ways paradox pulls me up and beyond my usual frame of reference into the bigger picture. But when I was first exposed to the idea that the world might not be as simple or as black and as I thought it was, I sometimes felt perplexed and vulnerable. It is natural that we would feel this way as our illusions and inadequate belief systems are challenged.

These are some examples of paradoxical thought:

- We are living and dying at the same time.
- We are individuals and we are all one.
- Doubt is part of the faith journey.
- Good leaders are servants.
- The more you learn, the more you realize how little you know.

How do we begin to wrap our minds around dichotomy? As the Greek origin of the word paradox (*para dokien* – "beyond thought") clarifies for us, these sorts of contradictions cannot be resolved by thinking about them. They are resolved through a willingness to entertain the notion that there are really no contradictions, but rather different perspectives of *one complete truth*.

As Patricia Spadaro explains in *Honor Yourself: The Inner Art of Giving and Receiving,*

"Our job, say the sages, is to learn to flow with the cadences of life as the universe asks us to bring first one and then the other side of the paradox to the fore in our lives at the right time and the right place. As an enlightened pundit once said, 'Blessed are the flexible, for they shall not be bent out of shape.'"

Wholeness and the shame-bind

My adult life has been a pilgrimage through the entanglement of childhood trauma into wholeness, freedom gained by inches. I have appreciated the ways that paradox and metaphor have helped me to see things more clearly. But there is one paradox that has played an especially important role. Along this journey I have discovered again and again that It is only through becoming aware and accepting of my weakness that I can find the strength of my authentic self.

One of the great challenges of my recovery has been confronting the issue of shame. I came to a place where, even with all the layers of healing I had attained, I was still in agony. It had reached a crisis point and could no longer be avoided. I felt inferior and insignificant, torturing myself with comparison—*I'm not as pretty, talented, skinny, creative, popular as they are, not as smart, not as cool, not as young, not as important, not as likeable.*

When I wasn't comparing myself to others, I was judging them, a constant whirlwind of negativity cycling through my mind—labelling others, jumping to conclusions, creating disparaging thoughts. The empathy and compassion I had was reduced to apathy. And social anxiety had begun to gain control. I didn't trust other people and I didn't feel okay enough to be around them.

I declared that I wanted out. I couldn't bear to live this way anymore. I had just heard the term "self-compassion" and felt led to do some research. It is said that when the student is ready the teacher appears, and appear it did. I was guided to the way out through an Internet search. There, like a flashing neon sign was the message: *The source of self-rejection is shame.*

Of course! I had read John Bradshaw's *Healing the Shame that Binds You* years ago. I knew what shame was, but identifying it in myself was difficult. The power of shame is its insidious nature. It is so inherent to our humanness that we often don't see it.

Shame's message is, "You are not enough, you are unworthy, you are a failure." Shame is at the heart of judgment and perfectionism. It keeps us self-absorbed, easily offended, contentious, and overly driven. Shame skews healthy boundaries and drives our fear of saying "no." I discovered, for example, that my people-pleasing was not really part of my inherent nature, but a shame-driven way to manipulate people into liking me so I might feel okay.

There are feelings of shame that are "often
unconscious and feel like inner ugliness... that if
others were to truly 'see' us, they'd recoil in scorn
or disgust," says Joseph Burgo
(afterpsychotherapy.com). Deep-seated shame is
often a result of childhood physical, emotional, and
sexual abuse. But feelings of unworthiness can also
be sparked by familial, cultural and social
expectations, often created and reinforced by
marketing and media.

Shame resilience and self-compassion

I have made it my mission to learn about shame
and its hold on my life. Regardless of the sources
of shame messages, I understand that I can
develop resilience to shame and open up to seeing
myself the way God sees me—not as a jumble of
defective parts, but as a *whole* person. I know I am
not impervious to shame, but I can take steps to
bounce back from those feelings and keep them

from disconnecting me from God, from myself, and from others.

Practicing shame resilience has opened space in my heart for self-compassion and I am noticing that empathy and compassion for others has begun to blossom and grow. I have found these steps from Brené Brown (brenebrown.com), researcher and author of books on vulnerability, courage, worthiness, and shame, to be very helpful in cultivating shame resilience:

1. Learn to recognize shame triggers and responses.
2. Speak about shame. Share experiences of shame with those I trust. Shame thrives in secrecy.
3. Challenge my "inner critic." Test negative self-talk with facts.
4. Delete the word *perfection* from my vocabulary.
5. Extinguish thoughts of comparison as they arise by using scripture or other messages that promote compassion toward myself.

Even though it can be difficult, it is imperative that I practice forgiveness—of myself for my inadequacies, of others when I feel disappointed. I must also be willing to ask for forgiveness when I've offended someone and then receive that forgiveness. The key word here is *practice*. The more I work with forgiveness, the less resistant I feel about giving and receiving it.

Compassion for myself involves wading deeply into my astounding and confounding humanness, holding tenderly my imperfection and vulnerability. As Kristen Neff (*Self-Compassion: Stop Beating Yourself Up and Leave Insecurity Behind*) writes, it means:

"to stop trying to label ourselves as 'good' or 'bad' and simply accept ourselves with an open heart. To treat ourselves with the same kindness, caring, and compassion we would show to a good friend—or even a stranger, for that matter...to allow life to be as it is."

It is a relief—and a real source of joy—to experience love flowing more freely in my life, nurturing the connections I want and deserve.

Imperfection and wholeness – a joyous paradox

"Imperfection is the very framework inside of which God makes the God-self known and calls us into gracious union. It's what allows us—and sometimes forces us—to fall into the arms of the living God." — Richard Rohr, OFM

For most of my life, I felt broken, defective—like there was something wrong with me. I felt different from everyone, the odd one out. I thought that that no one understood me. I felt lonely and alone.

What I didn't know back then was that *everyone* feels this way. Everyone (at one time or another and more often than not) experiences the feeling of being the odd person out, of feeling defective, of feeling alone. Our hearts get broken and we spend a lifetime mending them.

There have been plenty of times when I wondered if I would ever feel whole. I thought I might have to wait until I passed on to experience a sense of wholeness. To my surprise, I have discovered a marvelous paradox about what it means to be whole. I am beginning to understand *wholeness* as the state of being both fully human and fully connected to God (Love, our Source, the Divine, the Force, the infinite field of love and compassion).

When we love and accept ourselves as we are— even with our flaws and failings, our weaknesses and woundings—we are embracing the fullness of our humanity. As Richard Rohr says, my faults are *essential* to God's endeavors. The more human I am, the closer I connect to the divine that is present in and around me.

Certainly, we grieve our foibles and shortcomings. We regret opportunities we may have lost to show kindness or to practice tolerance or to listen—the times we fell short of loving well. Our hearts ache as we witness the consequences of choices made out of fear and in desperation, misery, misunderstanding, and ignorance. Yet, as we become more aware of our flaws and accept them as part of our humanity, we can use those flashes of consciousness to learn and grow—to think about how we might do it better next time. We can use our heartache to reach out to our Creator on behalf of others and to motivate ourselves to engage in the fight against injustices we see around us.

I have noticed a small shift taking place in myself as I've been confronting my quirks and embracing my shadow self (those aspects of self that are kept hidden in the dark and out of awareness). Now I chuckle to myself about the absurdity of some of my thoughts and responses. I forgive myself when I fall short. I give myself a little hug when I'm feeling down or vulnerable. As my ability to find compassion for myself grows, so to does my ability to tolerate the inadequacies of others. I feel less judgmental and seem to find grace a little more easily. It seems that as I've been opening up to myself, God's Spirit has been able to access more of me.

You see, we are perfect in our imperfection. Even in our brokenness, we are whole. The more fully human we are, the more full of love we become.

I wonder how much more compassion we would have for one another if we all understood this. I wonder how much more compassion we could have for each other if it was okay for us to share how vulnerable we all felt a lot of the time.

Waking Up

by Michele Stans

I was awake until 2010, then I fell asleep.

I was born into what I call The Jedi Family. Please forgive my #nerdgirl ways. I am a HUGE Star Wars fan. As I said: Jedi. I have it, my aunt has it and my grandma has it. My dad has it too but he pretends like he doesn't. He's a Mr. Spock engineer type and we all know there is a bit of a rift between Star Wars and Star Trek but, I digress.

When I was a child, I was blessed to not only be gifted intuitively but also musically. I was blessed to be surrounded by family who was also gifted and could guide me both by example and recommend courses of study. Even though I am the product of an engineer and an accountant, they too were open-minded but only so far as it didn't interfere with a good job and a 401k. I learned that one later in life.

When I was awake, I made leaps and followed my bliss. I moved from New York to Nashville to pursue a music career as a singer. It was awesome! I had a great time being the hot little number lead singer in a few bands, working as a demo singer and actually started taking on vocal students as a business. I wasn't making millions but I lived in a small apartment in the best area, the utilities were paid, I ate well and hung out with friends all the time. I was truly abundant.

Then I started listening to people tell me surely I was unhappy not having lots of stuff and money socked away. The life of a starving artist wasn't good for me. (Huh? I thought, "I'm not starving - I like my life...I don't understand.") I was told that I "needed to get my act together to be happy." These folks loved me so surely they were right...Right?

Even though those folks told me I would be happy going to law school, my soul just wouldn't let me.

So instead I got a secondary degree to my B.A. in communications in general practice law as a paralegal and I fell asleep.

I fell asleep to a lullaby that if I actually left my fulfilling, creative life in music and went to work in law, then I could get a good job with great benefits and a 401k, buy a three-bedroom, two-and-a-half bath home and have a sports car in the garage. Now THAT, the lullaby said, was joy. So I went to sleep.

My first wake up was in 2008 when my boyfriend and I lived in the hoity-toity-est zip code in Nashville. Here is what happened in the span of a month. I had gone to work at a TV network and found it wasn't a great fit, so my previous boss and I had decided I would come back to work for her in January. It was only October at this point but I was ok with floating for three months because I had made some money and I could always make money - I have a knack. So I quit the TV job. I was

blissfully unemployed for the next three months -
SQUEE! The next day, we were out looking at
houses because we wanted to move at the
beginning of the following year because we
wanted a bigger house. While out looking on a
beautiful, sunny afternoon, we were rear ended
and my car was demolished. Totaled. So now I
was jobless and carless. But I was ok - I could
handle that.

Within a week, I was at a hair appointment and my
boyfriend called because there was water pouring
by the gallon through our ceiling from the
apartment upstairs. My neighbor's water heater
had exploded while he was out of town and the
only person with a key was two hours away. Our
home was unlivable and needed full rehab. So I
was carless, jobless and homeless for the next
three months. Where was my lesson in this? I
sent out to the universe that I needed help. It sent
me insurance money, a fantastic contractor who
was honest and a blessing - and oddly we never

saw him again after our home was rebuilt. And it showed me I didn't need a car, job or home to be happy because my little family of my boyfriend, my dog and I always had a place to sleep and food to eat. We were good and moved back in three months later. And then I went back to sleep.

The next year, we bought a beautiful condo in a great neighborhood and had two German cars in the garage. And in May, 2010, Nashville saw the worst flood it had seen in nearly 100 years. We had four feet of water in our home...again. I woke up and asked the universe to help me again and legions of people sent money, help...and showed up. I can't even tell you how blessed we were. I was shown then that I was homeless again but never wanted for a place to sleep, food to eat or clothes to wear. In fact, we had run out of repair money and still had no staircase in the house. I had a talk with the universe and said, "We need $5000 to finish the house. I have no idea where we are going to get it so I am leaving that up to you and I know you will take care of us." I went to work that day and the phone rang - it was a local charity that knew we had flooded and said they had a check for me - wait for it - for $5000. I know I should've asked for five million. We rebuilt the house and I went back to sleep...well one eye was opened after this one.

In the next few years, my joy dwindled even more. I kept working in law and the universe kept sending me messages. My dog, who was my bestie for 14 years, transitioned across the rainbow bridge. I had her before I my boyfriend who became my life partner and she went through the two floods with me. Then my dad called; he had been diagnosed with cancer.

So in a decade we had two houses flooded, I changed jobs a bunch of times, my dog died and my dad was diagnosed. With all this going on, I didn't have time to even remember, much less

have an idea of what made me blissful or joyful -
much less how to find and follow it.

The next thing I knew it was 2014. Dad had been
cancer-free for four years, we adopted a new
puppy, I had the job, the house and the car they
promised would be my happiness. I could finally
breathe. I inhaled, exhaled and I woke up. I
looked around and YIKES! I asked myself, "Where
had my joy gone?" I was in a profession that really
didn't foster joy to pay for a sports car that spent
more time with the mechanic than me and ate out
so much I gained like a bazillion pounds. I was
unhappy, out of shape and confused because none
of the lullaby I was sung in my 20s was true. I was
now in my 40s and I had never been more
unhappy in my life.

I decided to start my journey back to myself. I was
talking to a neighbor who turned out to be a life
coach. She helped me spend a year rediscovering
who I was. One day, I realized I was here all along.
My spark was back. There's no place like home! I

just had to stop listening to everyone else's view of me, what THEY wanted me to be, and remember the beautiful view I had of myself.

I rediscovered my music and other creative outlets. I started my music studio up again and had to turn away students. I started back to my intuitive gifts and had clients asking me when they could come see me for a reading. I rebalanced. Both of these activities not only helped me follow and express my joy, it helped others. In my rebalancing I said to myself, "There are so many other people like me out there that I can help find their soul spark, their bliss! I can help them re-open their telephone lines to their soul so they can find their joy again."

I had always wanted to be someone who truly helped people embrace who they are as they are, and what better way than as a life coach, a vocal coach and an intuitive!

In my bag of bliss tricks that I carry with me, I have started making spiritually inspired jewelry to support people's spiritual energy and became a trained and certified Holistic Life Coach specializing in Law of Attraction. This way, I can use my own experience and journey back to my joy to encourage and support others in their journey to their own bliss and to live their best lives.

The universe is a funny thing. Even when you're not trying, it still wants to conspire for you to be aligned with your highest good. It may throw you some serious curve balls to show you just how strong you are and to remind you that it always has your back no matter what.

Vulnerability

A Four-Letter Word?

by Rebecca Carner

In today's society protection is paramount. Firewalls, passwords, personal safety, home security, homeland defense; the omnipresent messages are innumerable. The word 'vulnerability' strikes instantaneous fear in the hearts of many. Its connotation has equated it to a four-letter word.

From the Latin word 'vulnerabilis' whose root means, "to wound", *vulnerable* is a synonym to the words 'weak' or 'exposed' and therefore an antonym to the words 'protected' or 'strong'. Any and all vulnerability is therefore perceived as a threat to our security… and must be guarded against. So we oblige. We lock our doors. We password protect our bank accounts. We teach our children not to talk to strangers. We monitor our online presence. We encrypt our communications.

We do all these things to protect ourselves and our loved ones from all things harmful, all things threatening.

Externally, this practice is logical, pragmatic and necessary. To suggest anything different would be irresponsible. To leave oneself physically, financially, or electronically exposed is just a bad idea.

Internally, however, vulnerability is a very different experience. Managing emotional vulnerability is ultimately a completely separate practice. But many of us apply the exact same attitudes and actions to emotional vulnerability that we do to external vulnerability.

We are so trained through our interface with the outside world (which is now a 24/7 state of being) to recognize any perceived vulnerability and, with lightning speed, lock it away, that we don't allow for any exploration or understanding. All the things about ourselves that we deem to be 'vulnerable' are our weaknesses and therefore 'bad'. Through protecting ourselves in all the various ways that we do, we are attempting to make ourselves stronger, more secure, and, therefore, 'better'.

Locking away or hiding the 'bad' makes things 'good'... right?!? Unfortunately, no, it doesn't. And there lies the problem. Emotionally, when we do this we are cloistering away a piece of ourselves *from ourselves.* We think we are simply protecting ourselves, but we are limiting our own self-understanding and innate potential if we're not careful.

Similar to external vulnerability, we can easily pinpoint our emotional vulnerabilities because they bring up fear. They may be fears of loss, failure, abandonment, humiliation, inadequacy, despair, poverty, disreputableness, etc.

Think of a time when you felt emotionally vulnerable. It's important to consider a time when you felt it from the inside, not because you felt threatened or in danger from someone or something outside yourself. It may help to think of it as a time when you felt insecure, regardless of whether you expressed it or not. What were the circumstances?

Chances are you felt vulnerable during a time that you wanted or needed something. A time when you wanted something to ripen to full fruition or you needed something to go well, such as a romantic relationship potential, a job application, a scholarship or a grant, a creative project, a family gathering, a social event.

Now, instead of focusing on your fear of any possible negative result of that situation, think about what a potentially successful outcome looked like. Was it a new love, a new job, a degree you want, a beautiful work of art, a wonderful family reunion, a fun party? Consider why that was enticing to you. What would have been your gain? What is it about that positive result that would have felt good to you?

If we follow our external safety protocols and immediately lock our feelings away in an emotional vault, we have also put up an internal barrier as well. Because we fear loss, in whatever form it takes, we want to contain it and protect against it. But we are also effectively blocking the potential for a positive outcome as well. It reminds me of the Einstein quote, "You can't simultaneously prepare for war and plan for peace". You can't stand guard and welcome in at the same time. In our mad dash for safety and security, when we deny ourselves the opportunity to explore our feelings, we are also denying ourselves the opportunity to explore all of our possibilities.

Let's explore the example of the job application.

You have a job. It doesn't suit you for whatever reason(s). You see a listing for a position that you believe would suit you better. You apply for it.

Boom.

You feel vulnerable.

What if you don't get the job? What if you have to stay where you are? What if they don't hire you? You want the job but now you've realized you might not get it! Well, you can't tolerate that. Call in the defenses! They're going to smell fear in the interview so you need to lock up your feelings. You've got to make a good impression. You need to project strength and confidence.

It. Just. Happened.

You've both lost the opportunity to explore and understand your true feelings about changing jobs AND you may have very well sabotaged any chance of the interview going well.

Let's rewind a bit.

You have a job. It doesn't suit you fully. You see a listing for another position. You apply. You feel vulnerable. GREAT! (And yes, I actually mean that.) Open a question hotline in your mind with yourself.

Q: Why do you feel vulnerable?
A: Because I may not get the position. (*Loss you are trying to avoid*)

Q: Does that matter?
A: Yes because I want to leave my current job. (*What you actually want*)

Q: What don't you like about you current job?
A: I don't get to {fill in the blank} and it doesn't afford me enough {fill in the blank}. (*Why it's important to you*)

Q: Are those things the biggest reasons for you to leave?

A: Yes. (*Confirmation*)

Q: Does this new position have both of those things?

A: I think so but I'm not sure. (*You've set the fear aside, identified your needs/desires and now you need more information about the new opportunity*)

Q: Are those things you are going to ask in the interview?

A: Absolutely! (*Opening possibilities for an engaging and informative interview*)

Q: Do you think there are other jobs that would satisfy those needs?

A: Um, probably, I'm not sure. (*Because you've identified your true needs, you are open to the possibility that they can be met in many ways*)

Q: So if you don't get this job, could you research other opportunities for jobs that have what you are looking for?

A: Yeah, I sure could! (*Open to more potential*)

While this was a simplified version of all the considerations that go into making a job change, this example serves as a snapshot of the practice of exploring and understanding your true feelings. When you perceive vulnerability and immediately put it in an emotional vault, it literally locks away the possibility of any positive outcome. The fear exposed by that feeling of vulnerability creates a duality. In the first rendition/interpretation, the fear of not getting the job created the duality that you would either get the job (which would be 'good') or you wouldn't (which would be 'bad'). In the second rendition/interpretation, the duality evaporated. Through exploration and understanding, you identified what you want. Now, you realize that the job opportunity that you applied for may or *may not* have everything you want. You'll be more likely to present well in the interview because you will be assessing if it's what you want, not sitting there worrying that they may not hire you.

Additionally, whether you get that position or not, you now know exactly what you want and can seek it out in other positions. All of this would not have been possible if you had locked this 'vulnerability' away to 'protect' yourself. It is a false security and a false economy. You would not have 'saved' yourself from anything. You would have only blocked yourself from knowing what was important to you.

Ironically, through exploring and understanding your vulnerabilities, rather than banishing them, you have given yourself the ultimate protection against loss. Because you know what you need, you can pursue it until you achieve it. Whether it takes one job application or 20, you'll know you're fulfilling your needs. Anything and everything you try in the future will be taking you toward your goal.

As I wrote in my opening paragraph, "the word 'vulnerability' strikes instantaneous fear in the hearts of many." Vulnerability is perceived almost exclusively as a negative state. In most external situations, being vulnerable is perceived as negative because it indicates an undefended opening, a weak point. But within the internal emotional setting, being vulnerable is *positive* because such openings create an opportunity for deeper self-knowledge and understanding. Through exploring our feelings of vulnerability directly, rather than trying to lock them away, our potential is unblocked and more possibilities can present themselves. By dismantling our fears to see what was propelling them, we can discover our inner truths, our unique needs. When we know ourselves more fully it is much easier to effectively get what we need. By practicing self-actualization and understanding, we can create a new four-letter connotation for vulnerability...

Hope.

The Key to Finding Balance and Happiness in Your Life

by Stacey Melton

The key to finding balance between being happy, healthy and feeling good about life (all at the same time) for some folks may seem a bit challenging, me included. First things first...

Don't take things too serious. The situation you are experiencing is just that, an experience. Like everything in life, nothing is permanent. You have the power to change it if you want to.

Next...just practice gratitude. Be grateful for what you have...not just material things...ALL things. Write down five things every day that you are grateful for and refer back to them anytime you feel the need. Be grateful to those who do things for you.

Nourish your body. Eat a diet rich in fresh fruits and green vegetables every day. Drink lots and lots of clean water and exercise your body and mind everyday too. I would really like to go hiking in the Smoky Mountains. My plan is to do so. Gets me close to nature. Helps me reflect on the week and maybe see where I need to make positive changes in my own life or even help others do so.

Another thing to consider is asking for support. Having someone (like a life coach) in your life to be there for support and help keep you accountable with the things you want most out of life.

And whatever you do, don't forget to laugh. Laughter will always put you in an uplifted mood. I sometimes look in the mirror and start laughing at myself. I look so funny that I can't stop laughing. I literally crack myself up! Don't even really know what I am laughing at – haha. All I know is that it makes me feel good. And another thing - be positive with your words. Speak with words of empowerment and always stay positive. If you change the way you think, you change the way you live. Always think good thoughts.

And by all means, you owe it to yourself to commit. Whatever big thing you want in your life starts with changing small daily habits to get where you want to be. And don't forget to give yourself predictable time off when needed. Rest your mind from all the day-to-day obligations and chores. My husband and I enjoy our time together in the mornings before we head out to work. It gets us where we need to be so that we can live the day with gratitude and purpose.

Take several deep breaths every day. It helps to relax our inner self so that we can clear our minds and live the day to its full potential. And my favorite one - find your purpose. I say this because

I have just recently found my purpose in life. My purpose is to help people. You can find yours too. And not only do I help people, they help me too. I need them just as much as they need me. That is my gift in life, and we all are born with one. Make it a part of your daily chores to help someone every day. Recognize your gift and run with it. Living a radiant life comes from within. Remember you are important. You were born with the skills to live a radiant life.

Don't forget to eliminate as many toxins from your environment as possible. Take steps to protect yourself nutritionally and physically to help compensate for unavoidable exposure to heavy metals, herbicides, pesticides and even toxic people.

Minimize time-wasting activities such as watching TV excessively, engaging in video games or surfing the web. Life is too special to let precious hours slip away. Think to yourself, "How can I make a difference today?" and "Whose life can I touch or help change today?"

Know your personal style. When you understand and embrace your personal style, you'll live more confidently, letting your true self shine. No more pretending to be something you are not. I like to rock my own style. And you will be so surprised how everyone will notice it.

Think about ways to attain what's missing or eliminate what's unnecessary. This is where all our adventures take place. It will take some work as you step out of your comfort zone. And if anyone knows how uncomfortable that can be, it is ME. Adventures are scary to some people (me included) but very exhilarating if you commit to this step. You will no doubt feel how exciting life can be. For example, if you're looking for love, perhaps you'll let a trusted friend know that you would love to meet someone incredible. Maybe you would consider online dating. Maybe you'll go out on blind dates or try speed dating. I know it can be scary at first, but most likely it will get easier with practice.

The funny thing about being an active participant in building your beautiful radiant life is that it is full of surprises. I have found that things that I thought to be true about steps one, two and three, and four have changed. My assumptions were very wrong. By this time, you've likely gotten a taste of how beautiful life can be through adventures and new experience. Appreciate the little things in life. They are what matter most of all. Appreciate the little things that other people do for you. Sometimes they are the game changers - the moments in life when the tide turns and the perspectives change. I feel like the hardest thing to do sometimes is to ask for help. It's ok. People care about you and want to be there for you. Just ask them and you will see.

Enjoy as many moments of your life as is humanly possible. If there are only two moments each day, milk those two moments for all they are worth. My best moments are doing for others. These are precious moments to me. Even if they are rare. If you are fortunate to have more than two, then pass the love around. Other people could benefit from your positive outlook on life. I know in all my experience working with people, I find that my attitude and positivity are contagious to others around me. It makes everyone want to be around you, it brings out the best in people, and they truly learn to like themselves again.

If you don't feel that your life is beautiful right now, perhaps it's time to ask yourself what it is that you think is missing. Is it a purpose, inspiration, situation, happiness or something else? Whatever it is, none of these are good enough reasons to be unhappy or not live a beautiful and radiant life.

Life is beautiful! And even more so if you are living a life filled with happiness, peace and love without a soul full of anger, a job that sucks the life out of you, and an emptiness inside. I am one who felt a horrible emptiness most of my life - always feeling the need to run and not let myself be happy. We have to realize that we only get one chance at life, and the time is NOW. You are responsible for your happiness, and by following a few key elements and making a few changes you can too, just like me, live the most radiant possible.

There will be bumps, tears and heartache along the way as you shed and step into your truth, but you are worth it. I am worth it. It's time to say, "It's my life and I choose to take on the worthy life that is my birthright." The life that you dream about is residing in your heart and the answer to accessing this life is when you decide to say yes to going deeper.

It's the limitations in your mind that are holding you back. The limitation of unworthiness you have chosen to think and believe. As you push past these limitations and align your thoughts with love, you are moving toward the who you really are. Please learn to know thyself. You are worth it!

And last but not least, love, love and more love! Love is one of the things that makes life worth living. One of the things I have had to work on is that most of the time I expected love to be given to me in order for me to give it back. Instead of thinking this way, why not live your life with love being the main principle in all that you do especially when interacting with people in your day-to-day life. Everyone needs love in their life whether it's from a partner, a friend, family or even a pet. Make your beautiful life more meaningful by giving love to everyone you meet in the form of kindness, understanding, tolerance and generosity. I promise you that your life will be a radiant one - more than you could ever imagine.

Radiant Emails

by Tayla Scaife

It took me a while to see the advantages of Facebook, so I used email all the time. For years, I would send out inspiration emails to all of my friends or whoever would give me their emails. I decided to go back and do a compilation of some of those emails and share them with you. I have included the month and year. I hope you enjoy them as much as I did going back and reading them. I went ahead and threw in a couple of recent ones as well.

Take Action - November 2006

Today I want to share a few words with you, so that you will have a great day. Remember that today is just that TODAY. Yesterday has happened and tomorrow is not here yet. Enjoy the day that you have been blessed to see. Tell the people that are in your life that you love them. If you are confused about any aspect of your life, decide whether or not you have control. If you don't give it to God to take care of and if you have control look deep inside of yourself and find the solution. Don't ponder, take action. I want to let each and every one you know that you have the power to conquer all. God has given you that power. Use it and find your way.

The Game of Tunk - December 2006

My husband and I play cards all the time together. One of our favorite games is Tunk. In the game of Tunk you are dealt 7 or 9 cards. Then the deck is placed on the table. You are given the choice to throw a card out of your hand and pick another from the deck. After you have the hand that is suited for you to win you make a spread. It is the same with life. Life is a lot like the game of Tunk. There has always been the saying that, "These are the cards that we are dealt." That is not all that true. We are given certain opportunities in life and you are given the chance to make choices. You can decide whether or not a certain circumstance is going to be good for you or you can let it go and another chance will come your way. This will happen over and over again until you find the correct combination to make your life as happy as it can be. It is all about choices. We all have them. It is up to each of us to decide whether or not those choices are the best for us and our situation.

How will you choose to live today? - April 2007
How will you choose to live today? Will you choose to allow those weapons that have formed to prosper? Will you live by a defeated mentality? Will you say today I give up, it is not worth it?
Or
Will you choose to live like today as if it is the last day you will ever see? Will you do something differently today than yesterday? Will you take the time to check your priorities?

How will you choose to live your life, just for today? We can only worry about today because tomorrow is not promised. We can only worry about this particular second because the next one is not promised. Don't take the day for granted. It can be good to you. Only if you choose to make the best day you have ever had.

Perspective - June 2007

Your perspective has everything to do with every situation in your life. According to dictionary.com, perspective means the ability to perceive things in their actual interrelations or comparative importance. In order to have a positive experience in life you must have positive thoughts. To have positive thoughts you must look at all situations at all angles. If you are having a bad day at work and your boss or coworker is hitting that last nerve you can look at it one or two ways. You can be thankful that you have a job and that your purpose on that job is greater than anyone that works there or you can allow them to have control of your day. If a person cuts in front of you as you drive you can look it at it one or two ways - Be glad that you did not rear end them, that both of you are safe, and pray that they make it to their journey safely or you can cuss and get angry only to raise your stress level. Once again it is all about how you look at the situation. Your perspective is your truth. I challenge you to look at a particular situation in a positive way and see if it makes a difference.

The Man with the Cart - June 2008

I was on my way to work when I saw a homeless man. I have seen him many times before, but today was a little different. I was not in a rush and did not have other things on my mind. I was present and observing everything around me.

I noticed that he was pushing a shopping cart. I started to look a little harder and longer to see what he was carrying. There was a full-size mattress - yes I said mattress. There was bag tied to the back of it and I really could not see anything else.

Two things occurred to me as I watched him push

that buggy with all of his strength. There were a lot of people like him. People who are carrying all this stuff with them from the past. They are not able to move as efficiently because they have all this STUFF holding them back. They are not able to let go and because they don't know how to live in the moment they continue to hold resentments, which turns into anger. LET IT GO AND LIVE!

The second thing that occurred to me is that this man has everything he owns in a shopping cart. Every solitary thing he owns is in a shopping cart. All of the clothes he has is probably on his back. Most of us have one or more of the following things:

A home full of furniture

A job

A car

Clothing

Food (or access to it at any moment)

A computer

Television

Ironing board

Washer and Dryer

Water

Radio

YOUR RIGHT MIND - September 2008

You get the picture! You have so much to be
grateful for. Stop waiting on that thing to come (a
partner, the right job, the degree, weight loss, etc.)
you think you need in order to start living your
life. It is a LIE. All you need is to make the decision
that you are going to live your life to the fullest. It
may never come and you will still be waiting. Life
is a gift only if you choose for it to be. It is a
beautiful thing if you change your perspective. The
man and the shopping cart is a lesson to all of us.
Be grateful and be thankful for where you are. You
are where you are supposed to be because that is
where you are in this moment. LIVE LIFE

Understanding - August 2008

Today I will talk about understanding. The author

Byron Katie says it best. She believes that it is not up to others to understand you, but for you to understand yourself.

Do many of you worry about what other people think of you or say to yourself, "People just don't understand me." Believe it or not it is not your responsibility to "get others" or for them to "get you". They are who they are and you will waste so much time trying to figure them out. You should take that time to understand your personality, your likes and dislikes. It is ultimately your decision to begin to accept your own opinions of yourself. When you began to take a look at other people you must first look at yourself. That is how you began to stand on your own two feet and be comfortable in your skin and your own beliefs.

People will always have an opinion of you, but what is your opinion of yourself? At the end of the day that is all that matters. You have to be with you 24 hours a day.

One last thing, please think about this before you do it next time. Think really hard when you ask someone for their opinion of something. A lot of times we have our own conclusions and when we ask others theirs we hear what we don't want to hear. I learned that from my momma. I have learned from her that if I need you just to listen I voice that no matter who it is. When I am ready to hear a person's opinion I ask for that. In the end you will have made your own decision based on your thoughts and how you feel.

Right Direction - November 2015
There is something about being headed in the right direction. About finally understanding what you believe, what you want, what you deserve, who you are and accepting it all. Not being afraid of what others are going to say, do or think. Being able to make the decision that is best for you because you finally embrace your journey. There is such peace in that. Such peace in knowing that no matter what happens you are good. That you are

taken care of and protected. That it is always going to work out. Putting your trust in what you believe and moving without knowing what is going to happen. There is peace and freedom it that. There is no need for the labels and stress. It is all going to go as it is supposed to. That is living.

I Never Thought - November 2015

I never thought I could fall in love with myself. I never thought I would find love outside of men. I never thought I would be ok by myself. I never thought I would not be depressed or anxious. I never thought I would be able to just be. I never knew how to achieve these things on my own. I just did not know how. Well I found out all I had to do was look myself in the mirror and deal with me. Take responsibility for it all. The hurt, the pain, the not forgiving, my attitudes and beliefs towards certain things, people, and situations, the things that no longer served me. I grieved the old me and welcomed the new one. What an amazing journey. What an amazing ride. Now it is time to start the (heart) work, but I will need to work like I never have before to get where I need to be.

They Gotta GO - November 2015

The way to get toxic people, energy vampires, liars, manipulators, con artist, abusers, or people you just don't want in your life is to realize they really do not exist. All of the behavior was created in your mind when you started to accept it for just that. Don't try to see them in a different light, as a different color, as what you "want" them to be. They will not change. They are not going to change. What purpose do they serve? Then get bold enough to call them out on their shit. Oh yes, start asking questions. Make them answer you. They will run like hell. Send the questions in writing, so they have to answer. They will trip up. When you start to ask questions and confront them you take your power back, you take your energy back. They cannot survive. Try it. I bet it will work and you will feel like you can take on the world.

ABOUT THE AUTHORS

More information on these
Holistic Coach co-authors
is available at
RadiantCoaches.com